CW01095055

"*The Activator Advantage* is a must-read for professional services leaders who want to grow their businesses. In an increasingly unpredictable marketplace, where clients are facing constant upheaval, we can't expect the same approaches to deliver similar, much less better, results. This new research introduces business development for the future—and it is proactive engagement, collaboration, creating value, and never, ever getting comfortable."

 —**CONSTANTINE ALEXANDRAKIS,** CEO, Russell Reynolds Associates

"*The Activator Advantage* demystifies the 'dark art' of professional services selling. Backed by a first-of-its-kind research study into the mindsets and behaviors of the best professional services business developers, the book provides a road map for those in work-winning roles. We are seeing real results at our firm from following the Activator approach."

 —**RAYA BLAKELY-GLOVER,** Global Head of Business Development
  and Sales, Bird & Bird

"B2B sales concepts often fail to land in professional services firms, and *The Activator Advantage* shows you why. An invaluable guide on how to sell—and more importantly, how to build genuinely fruitful client relationships—in professional services today. Using research-backed data purely from professional services, *The Activator Advantage* is a game changer for those professionals who have long wished to get over the 'ick' factor of business development and build stronger, more meaningful client relationships."

 —**SOPHIE BOWKETT,** Chief Marketing Officer, Bird & Bird

"A blueprint for mastering business development in professional services, *The Activator Advantage* blends data-driven research with practical strategies to help you drive consistent results in today's competitive client landscape."

 —**MARK COPELAND,** former Chief Commercial Officer, Accordion

"*The Activator Advantage* offers invaluable insights into proactive client engagement, robust networking, and delivering multifaceted value. An essential for those professionals aiming to elevate their client service strategies and achieve exceptional results."

—**ERIN CORBIN MESZAROS**, Global Business Development
and Marketing Officer, Eversheds Sutherland

"*The Activator Advantage* offers a practical framework for professionals aiming to build client relationships and expand their practices. It offers actionable strategies based on research and data applied to industry-specific insights and helps professionals develop the mindset and confidence to create value for clients and forge successful collaboration with their colleagues."

—**SAMUEL DANON**, Managing Partner, Hunton Andrews Kurth

"'What do top rainmakers do differently?' is one of the most debated questions in our profession. DCM Insights has answered the question with data—not opinion. *The Activator Advantage* is now the go-to framework for business development at our firm. We have already seen the positive impact this new approach has had."

—**HELEN DRAYTON**, CEO, Penningtons Manches Cooper

"From the moment I read 'What Today's Rainmakers Do Differently' in *Harvard Business Review*, I saw the Activator approach as essential to the modern professional services landscape. In today's competitive market, building proactive networks, creating value, and collaborating across teams define success."

—**DANIEL KNOLL**, National Industry Leader, Financial Services,
KPMG Australia

"Boomer and Gen X professionals had *The Trusted Advisor* as required reading. Millennials and Gen Z should have *The Activator Advantage*. It's that good."

—**PAUL LEWIS**, Firmwide Managing Partner, Linklaters

"Practical and compelling. . . . *The Activator Advantage* provides a case for change and a path forward for any firm recognizing the need to aggressively leverage the entirety of its talents to differentiate service, impact, and lasting value."

—**SCOTT McINTYRE**, CEO, Guidehouse

"Business development in professional services organizations is different from sales in other sectors, but that doesn't mean that the levers and attributes of high performance can't be isolated, replicated, and scaled. But doing this effectively is a matter of deep analysis and rigorous inquiry. *The Activator Advantage* distills the output of such work into tangible takeaways for individuals, teams, and leaders to grow ever more valuable client relationships."

—**TOM MONAHAN**, CEO, Heidrick & Struggles

"I commend the DCM Insights team for their excellent research inspiring professionals to leverage technology to better manage client relationships. *The Activator Advantage* is vital reading—useful and thought provoking—offering tools and tactics to enhance competitiveness."

—**JOHN MURPHY**, National Managing Partner and CEO,
Borden Ladner Gervais

"*The Activator Advantage* is a pivotal resource for B2B professionals serious about business development. Backed by cutting-edge research and real-world success stories, it delivers actionable strategies to build lasting client relationships, close more deals, and fuel sustainable growth. An imperative title for anyone striving for top-tier performance."

—**LAURA NICHOLLS**, Chief Client Officer, Clifford Chance

"*The Activator Advantage* is a revolutionary book, providing a research-backed programmatic system for revenue growth in professional services. It is effective because it accounts for some of the significant differences in professional services firms versus other B2B organizations. Buy this book if you're in professional services and looking for a blueprint for organic growth."

—**ANGELA PETROS,** Global Chief Marketing Officer,
  Baker McKenzie

"For any professional interested in becoming a better rainmaker, this book is necessary reading. It's the only book of its kind that's evidence-based, aimed specifically at professionals, and as readable as a novel."

—**LARRY RICHARD,** founder, LawyerBrain

"This excellent book does a fantastic job of bringing to life the authors' compelling research into the Activator rainmaker in a practical, tactical, and absorbing way."

—**ADAM SOAMES,** Global Chief Business Development Officer,
  Ashurst

"*The Activator Advantage* is crucial for leaders of professional services firms looking to foster collaboration to drive sustainable growth in today's rapidly changing marketplace."

—**PATRICK WALSH,** CEO, Withum

"As a CMO in a big law firm, I am inundated with approaches on how to maximize ROI. But one constant has remained the key to increasing law firms' profits and client relationships (and how we develop, grow, and sustain them). *The Activator Advantage* helps our lawyers discover the clear map of priorities they need to implement in a thoughtful and intentional way while allowing them to cut out the behaviors that are not successful in building and sustaining meaningful, growing client work. Using data and practical, real-world examples, the DCM Insights team provides a succinct and approachable guide to help today's lawyers discover the habits they need to cultivate in order to be successful in this competitive landscape."

—**TIFFANY ZEIGLER,** Chief Marketing Officer, Polsinelli

"At a moment when we crave meaningful connection and relationships, not division, the DCM Insights team delivers a powerful follow-up to their prior work in *The Activator Advantage*. These principles provide guidelines for advisors looking to revitalize their practices and find more meaning in their careers. This book has been groundbreaking for our rising stars, helping them understand what our most successful partners do. For leaders, it provides the data and vocabulary to coach their teams in a way they instinctively know makes sense. It's truly one of those 'theories of everything' that professionals are seeking right now."

—**MITCH ZUKLIE,** Chairman and CEO, Orrick

The
Activator
Advantage

The
Activator

WHAT TODAY'S
RAINMAKERS DO
DIFFERENTLY

Advantage

MATTHEW DIXON · RORY CHANNER
KAREN FREEMAN · TED McKENNA

HARVARD BUSINESS REVIEW PRESS
BOSTON, MASSACHUSETTS

Copyright 2025 DCM Insights

All rights reserved

Printed in the United States of America

10 9 8 7 6 5 4 3 2 1

The web addresses referenced in this book were live and correct at the time of the book's publication but may be subject to change.

Library of Congress Cataloging-in-Publication Data

Names: Dixon, Matthew, author.
Title: The activator advantage : what today's rainmakers do differently / Matthew Dixon, Rory Channer, Karen Freeman, Ted McKenna.
Description: Boston, Massachusetts : Harvard Business Review Press, [2025] | Includes index.
Identifiers: LCCN 2024044155 (print) | LCCN 2024044156 (ebook) | ISBN 9798892790574 (hardcover) | ISBN 9798892790581 (epub)
Subjects: LCSH: Business. | Economic development.
Classification: LCC HF1008 .D59 2025 (print) | LCC HF1008 (ebook) | DDC 650—dc23/eng/20250118
LC record available at https://lccn.loc.gov/2024044155
LC ebook record available at https://lccn.loc.gov/2024044156

ISBN: 979-8-89279-057-4
eISBN: 979-8-89279-058-1

The paper used in this publication meets the requirements of the American National Standard for Permanence of Paper for Publications and Documents in Libraries and Archives Z39.48-1992.

To the Activators

Contents

Preface

A Different Kind of Selling

Back in 2012, I was invited to present the results of a global study of business-to-business (B2B) sales professionals to a large strategy consulting firm at their annual partner retreat. I received a warm welcome from the four hundred partners in the audience, but my presentation of our research seemed to fall flat almost immediately. The audience wasn't as engaged as others had been. I'd presented this material countless times to organizations around the world, but I could tell that this group of consultants wasn't buying it.

My talk was planned for sixty minutes but at the forty-five-minute mark, the managing partner of the firm, who was seated in the front row along with the firm's other executive leaders, stood up and started waving his arms, signaling that I should stop the presentation. This had never happened to me before.

"I was going to take questions in just a few minutes, but please, go ahead," I said. The managing partner gestured for a handheld microphone from one of the staff working the event and then said—in front of the entire room—"I'm sorry to interrupt. This is all very interesting, but there seems to have been some miscommunication when we hired you to present to us." "OK," I said, "What was the misunderstanding?" He replied, "You've spent the past forty-five minutes talking about sales effectiveness, salespeople, and best practices in selling. It's fascinating research, and I'm sure many of our clients would be very interested in it, but I don't see how it's relevant to the people in this room. We're not salespeople. We don't do sales. In fact, we don't *sell* anything here."

I'd never heard this before and was at a loss for words. I recalled a story shared with me by Professor Neil Rackham, author of *SPIN Selling* and the person generally regarded as the godfather of modern professional sales. When I first met him many years ago, he shared a similar experience. He'd been challenged on the relevance of his work to an audience of professional services partners. His response seemed like the right thing to say in front of the audience that had turned on me.

"I understand," I said, "but can we stipulate to the fact that there is a mysterious process by which your clients' money ends up in your firm's bank account . . . and can we just call it 'sales' for now?"

The room burst into laughter, suddenly breaking the permafrost layer that I'd been trying to pierce since the beginning of my session. The managing partner laughed and said, "Fair enough. Go ahead and finish your presentation."

In the hallway after my session, one of the firm's senior partners pulled me aside. He seemed to take pity on me for what was clearly an awkward experience. He explained that the group had a deep aversion to the "S word," as he called it. "Sales," he explained, "has a very pejorative connotation around here."

I assumed that this was rooted in some sort of intellectual snobbery; after all, most professionals have MBAs, JDs, and other advanced degrees from prestigious universities. Many had spent time as senior executives at some of the biggest companies in the world. And who could blame them? The perception people have of salespeople—one largely shaped by Hollywood depictions in movies like *Glengarry Glen Ross, Boiler Room,* and *The Wolf of Wall Street*—isn't exactly positive.

But it turns out that this wasn't the real reason the firm's partners had such an allergic reaction to being called salespeople. It's because, in many fundamental ways, they are *not* salespeople. The job of professionals like consultants, lawyers, and accountants, he explained, is fundamentally different from that of a typical salesperson. And so it offends professionals—who are, as a group, trained to be detail-oriented, data-driven critical thinkers—to call them something they're not. Unfortunately, the partners in his firm and, he suspected, the partners of most firms, have long been skeptical of sales experts like me. Over the years, leadership had brought in numerous experts to improve the commercial effectiveness of the firm's professionals. Their intentions may have been good, but the relevance of their teaching was not. In the end, despite spending significant sums on sales training, he told me, they had not seen any real change in behavior or tangible improvement in results.

Unlike B2B commercial organizations in which demand generation, sales, product delivery, customer success, and account management are discrete functions and roles, professionals are responsible for doing *all* of these jobs, often by themselves with little support from their firms. As *doer-sellers*, professionals own the entire business development and service delivery lifecycle: they must build awareness of their own expertise in the market to generate demand, identify and close new client business, deliver the work to the client, and then renew and expand the relationship over time.

Not only are the responsibilities of a professional different from those of a salesperson, but the nature of the commercial relationship is different. In most sales organizations, the commercial process is linear. Marketing generates a lead and hands it to the salesperson to close. Like an assembly line, once a deal is signed and a new client is secured, the salesperson passes it on to the team responsible for implementing the solution and ensuring that the customer gets value out of it. And then the process starts over, with the salesperson moving onto the next lead they're handed. By contrast, because a professional does all of these jobs, their commercial relationships with clients are circular in nature. They bring new clients on, deliver the work that was sold to them, and then look to renew those relationships—continuing to do the same type of work for the client or finding opportunities to expand the relationship. The relationship between the B2B salesperson and a customer is momentary, usually starting and ending within a few months. But the relationship between a professional and their client can (and should, in most cases) last years, even decades.

Finally, the relationship between professionals and their firms is unique—wholly different from the one that exists between a seller and her employer. Salespeople work for a company and it is expected that they will sell the way their employer requires. They use messaging, tools, collateral, and even sales techniques prescribed by the companies they work for. And their performance is rewarded with commissions on deals they close. Partnerships, on the other hand, are typically democracies. Firms provide training, technology, and enablement to their professionals to support their commercial efforts but are ultimately powerless to make their professionals use any of these resources. If a professional decides to do things differently, there isn't much a firm can do to tell them otherwise. Partners in professional services firms *own* the business, they don't *work for* the business. And they aren't paid commissions but instead receive a share of the firm's profits. But the biggest difference between salespeople and other professionals is that salespeople sell a product. In professional services, the professional *is* the product. They are selling their advice, experience, and expertise—not a piece of software or other manufactured product—to the client.

I left that conference with a new appreciation for the unique role professionals play in the growth of their firms. And an appreciation for the fact that, despite conducting years of research into what makes salespeople tick, very little of what I knew was relevant to this—one of the largest sectors of the global economy.

So I did what any good researcher would do in this situation. I spent the next decade dodging invitations to speak at partner retreats. After all, our research team had nothing of value to say to this audience.

Until now.

—Matthew Dixon
Washington, DC
February 2024

Introduction

The Rainmaker Genome Project

For as long as the professional services industry has existed, its growth—not to mention its survival during periods of economic downturn—has revolved around a single core tenet: *if you do good work and develop a strong relationship with your clients, they will come back to you the next time they need support.*

This belief has driven nearly every aspect of the way professionals operate—from how they spend their time to how they manage their books of business, engage with clients, pitch for new work, collaborate (or not) with their colleagues, and differentiate themselves from competitors. It also underpins the operating model of nearly every professional services firm. For instance, it governs critical decisions around who is elected to partner, which lateral hires to bring into the firm, and how year-end bonuses are allocated. Despite the differences that exist between industries like law, accounting, consulting, investment banking, public relations, executive search, architecture, design, engineering, marketing, and advertising, to name just a few, this belief has long been the axis on which the professional services industry spins.

But there is a growing problem with this belief, one that is rarely discussed openly, even at the highest levels of the biggest firms in the world: clients, even long-standing ones for whom firms have delivered unquestioned value in the past, are much less loyal than they once were.

A survey of one hundred C-level buyers conducted by our firm, DCM Insights (DCMi), found that the social compact that once existed between professionals and their clients is fraying, perhaps irreparably. When asked the extent to which they agreed or disagreed with the statement, "Provided the professional or firm we used in the past delivered good work, we would be inclined to hire them again if a new need arose," their responses were eye-opening. Seventy-six percent of participants told us that as recently as five years ago, they would have agreed or strongly agreed with this sentiment. Today, however, only 53 percent of these senior buyers reported that going back to the same professionals for repeat work was a given. And a mere 37 percent were willing to say that their preference five years from now would be to automatically engage the same service provider again.

There are numerous reasons for this shift. Purchasing in "soft-spend" categories like professional services, once a black box shielded from corporate procurement departments, is rapidly becoming more formalized. Not only has this put pressure on incumbent firms to compete for business they once received automatically, but it's opened the door to direct competitors as well as boutique and niche players previously outside of the consideration set. It's also given rise to alternative fee structures—such as fixed fees, capped fees and performance-based fee models—as procurement looks to extract more value for money from the firms they work with. What's more, most segments in professional services have seen new, disruptive entrants show up in recent years. These alternative service providers have not just siphoned off low-value, transactional work from top-tier players but are now starting to compete for higher-end projects as well, a trend that is likely to accelerate dramatically in the next few years as AI automates work that was once the bread and butter of many professional services firms.

Hearing professionals describe what it's like trying to develop client business in today's market is painful. One Big Four consulting partner told us that she recently lost a significant piece of work to a boutique player she'd never competed against before:

> We've been the go-to provider for this client for years. Because of the quality of the work we've delivered and the strength of our relationship, I've never really had to sell to them. They would just automatically reach out anytime they needed help. So, needless to say, I was in a bit of shock when I heard through the grapevine that they'd gone with another firm for work that we are well equipped to deliver. The most baffling part to me was that when I called to ask them if we'd done something wrong, they seemed just as surprised that I would even think that. "No!" they exclaimed, "You guys are great! We love working with you! You're the best consulting team we've ever worked with!" Suffice it to say, it was deeply troubling to me to think that we'd done everything right and still lost.

The impact on the professional services industry has been dramatic. While top performers seem to be figuring out how to grow their books of business in this more competitive and challenging client-buying environment, average performers are falling further and further behind. What was once an 80-20 problem for most firms—where the top 20 percent of professionals drive 80 percent of the organization's growth—has become a 90-10 problem, if not worse. Firm leaders have been shaken out of their comfort zones and are scrambling for answers. In a recent report from PwC Law, for instance, providing commercial training to partners was ranked as the number one strategy for driving organic growth and profit margin for the top hundred law firms worldwide— even higher than investing in new technologies like AI, over which significantly more ink has been spilled. Seventy-three percent of these firms reported that they are pursuing business development training for their partners, and the remaining 27 percent reported that they were considering investments in this area.[1]

It was into this disruptive environment that our team at DCMi partnered with Intapp, a cloud software provider to professional and financial services firms around the world, to launch a massive research study that we dubbed "the Rainmaker Genome Project." Our goal: to conduct the first-ever quantitative study of professionals to identify, with data, what makes today's top business developers different from their peers.

For close to two years, we recruited firms and their professionals. In our initial sample, we collected detailed data on nearly three thousand partner-level professionals across more than forty law, accounting, consulting, investment banking, public relations, and executive search firms. We asked them about nearly every aspect of their business development approaches: their attitudes toward it, how they spend their time, how they choose client opportunities to pursue, how they use internal resources, how they engage clients, and other activities. We then collected performance data on every professional who responded and ran in-depth, structured behavioral interviews with the top eighty business developers we identified. These interviews helped us to understand not just *what* they do, but *how* they do it—and even more importantly. wh⋯ they do the things that they do. Finally, we took this data a series of sophisticated statistical analyses.

What emerged from this research was something entirely ι

We discovered that all professionals could be placed into business development profiles: Experts, Confidants, Debater and Activators. In and of itself, this was a startling finding, es light of the decades-old management guidance that every profes either a "finder, minder, or grinder"—a framework that, while tedly convenient, is overly simplistic, if not misleading. Being seller in professional services, it turns out, is a far more comp business. For the first time, we were able to give professional se. leaders a data-driven way to think about the makeup of their firms, ι professionals themselves a research-backed explanation for how th own business development approaches differ from those of their peers.

But a bigger surprise was yet to come.

When our team compared the relative business development performance of these five profiles, we found that many of the most common behaviors are, in fact, negatively correlated with performance. Nearly

80 percent of all professionals in our study have chosen business development approaches that aren't just *unproductive* in today's client buying environment, they're *counterproductive*.

Instead, we found that only one of the five identified profiles had a positive statistical impact on performance. Whether these professionals chose to ignore the conventional wisdom or simply found that it didn't work for them is unclear. But what was apparent is that they have taken an approach that is altogether unique and undeniably more effective.

What makes their approach so different?

First, while most professionals continue to pursue a business development approach predicated on the idea that doing good work is in itself the most effective form of business development, these top performers see this as table stakes—necessary but entirely insufficient to be a successful growth-oriented business developer. These talented professionals eschew the conventional wisdom in favor of a radically different approach. Rather than performing business development intermittently when client work allows, these professionals do so *consistently*, with a near-metronomic cadence that would make any professional salesperson jealous. Second, instead of building protective moats around their clients designed to insulate them from others, these professionals actively *collaborate*. They are super-connectors, purposefully building bridges that connect clients with colleagues and others in their professional networks who they know will deliver value. And, finally, rather than *taking* business opportunities—waiting for clients to recognize they have a need that requires the support of a professional services firm—these professionals *make* their own business opportunities by proactively engaging clients with new ideas to mitigate risk, cut costs, and grow the topline of their businesses.

We call these top performers *Activators*, and this book is their story.

– 1 –

Why Activators Win

Whenever we gather professionals to go through our Activator training program, the very first thing we do is engage in a group discussion about the current client buying environment. When asked what one word best describes what it's like to try to win client work in today's market, the responses—no matter whether it is a group of lawyers, accountants, consultants, executive recruiters or investment bankers—are as consistent as they are troubling: "difficult," "challenging," "painful," "competitive," "unpredictable," "tough," "hard."

And the pain is felt not just at the front lines. Firm leaders report warning signs as well: an increase in request for proposal (RFP)-driven purchasing; a slowdown in repeat business from key clients; and pressure on rates, billable hours, and advisory fees. Perhaps most troubling is a widening spread between high performers and core performers, which has increased the urgency in understanding what top performers are doing differently to be successful in a much more challenging client buying environment.

Industry experts have been sounding the alarm for some time now. In a recent report, researchers at the Thomson Reuters Institute issued a warning to firms:

> [L]eaders can choose to ignore these changes but . . . they do so at their peril. To be sure, embracing the new market realities

will be challenging as they run counter to many of the instincts, training, and experience that many . . . hold. What is required, however, is an openness to new ways of thinking about structuring the delivery of . . . services in a market that no longer rewards many of the traditional ways of doing things. . . . Those who do not, will . . . leave their organizations ill-equipped and vulnerable to the vagaries of the marketplace, often offering the wrong services in the wrong ways and wondering why nothing they do is working like it used to.[1]

One head of M&A advisory at a leading global investment bank told us, "Even longtime clients who've spent millions of dollars with us and have never gone to any of our competitors are now forcing us to compete for their business." The CBDO (chief business development officer) of a top accounting firm reported, "The gap between [our] top performers and our average performers is widening at a dramatic rate." And the CMO (chief marketing officer) of an Am Law 100 firm said bluntly, "Clients today are a lot less loyal than they used to be."

It was with this backdrop of a fast-changing client buying environment that we launched our study into what today's rainmakers do differently.

Five Types of Professionals

While there has been a significant amount of research on what differentiates top-performing salespeople from their peers—including several major studies conducted by the authors of this book—there has been little to no real research done on professional services, which represent a unique go-to-market model in the B2B landscape.[2] All of the seminal works in the industry provide robust frameworks and guidance to professionals but are, unfortunately, based largely on anecdotal evidence or the personal experiences of the authors. What's more, these pieces haven't been updated to reflect today's client buying realities.

FIGURE 1-1

Sample and study overview

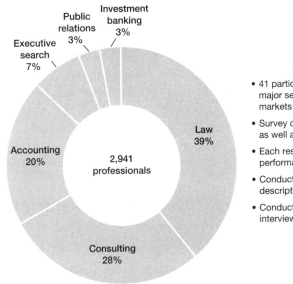

Public relations 3%

Investment banking 3%

Executive search 7%

Accounting 20%

2,941 professionals

Law 39%

Consulting 28%

Study overview

- 41 participating firms across all major segments and geographic markets
- Survey covered 108 total attributes as well as a set of control variables
- Each respondent's firm provided performance data
- Conducted factor, regression, and descriptive analyses on the data
- Conducted 60-minute behavioral interviews with 83 top performers

Our team at DCMi decided to change this by conducting the first global, data-based study designed to understand what makes top-performing business developers different from their peers in the professional services industry. (See figure 1-1 for an overview of the study. More details about the methodology are available in the appendix.)

Our first surprising finding came from the factor analysis we performed on the data. Factor analysis is a statistical method that looks at how, in a large dataset, different variables naturally "clump" together and move together as a unit in a model, potentially surfacing a smaller set of latent patterns or unobserved variables. This technique helps researchers reduce a large dataset into a simple, understandable, and digestible story. It's been applied in a variety of fields, from product management to psychometrics and personality psychology.

Our analysis revealed that every one of the professionals we studied could be placed into one of five distinct, statistically defined profiles: Experts, Confidants, Debaters, Realists, and Activators (see figure 1-2).

FIGURE 1-2

The five types of professionals

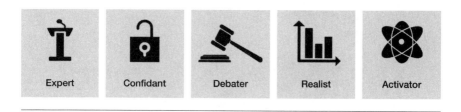

| Expert | Confidant | Debater | Realist | Activator |

We'll go through each of them in detail but, before we do, a few words of caution.

First, while professionals can (and typically do) possess attributes from multiple profiles, each respondent in our study could be placed into one of them. In other words, every professional "spikes" in one of these five business development approaches, even if they have trace characteristics of others. Some professionals will immediately identify with one of the five, while others will feel that they're split between two or more, but statistically, every professional majors in one profile.

Second, a common reaction to this finding is believing that these profiles are effectively personality types. But it's important to point out that we did not study personality traits. Why? Because personality isn't something that can be changed. We chose instead to focus on attributes like skills, behaviors, time spend, resource utilization, mindsets, and so on. These are things that *can* be changed with the right training, coaching, and support from the organization. Of course, there is a separate, but related, question about why an individual would choose one approach over another, and likely part of that choice has to do with their personality. But, as we'll discuss later, there are other powerful factors at play that influence a professional's choice about how to engage clients: a firm's compensation model, its cultural norms, messaging from leadership, mentorship and coaching from established rainmakers, and pervasive conventional wisdom about what makes for effective client engagement.

As we go through each of these profiles in detail, we'll share some of the variables that factor together to describe each of these different professionals—as well as some of the color commentary gleaned through our interviews.

The Expert

The Expert is best described as the reluctant business developer—far more comfortable doing the work than selling the work (see figure 1-3 for a summary). For some, this aversion can come across as contempt for what they perceive to be an unfortunate, but necessary, evil of their profession. One partner from a large global law firm declared boldly, "I didn't go to law school to become a salesperson." For others, it's because business development feels unseemly. One Expert we spoke to stated that he didn't enjoy business development because "People only have to sell when they don't believe in the inherent value they deliver. If what you do is truly valuable, clients will seek you out and ask to pay for your services." Because of this distaste for the commercial side of the job, Experts tend to adopt a reactive business development posture—waiting for a prospective client to find them, recognize their unique expertise, and reach out to them for their services.

FIGURE 1-3

The Expert profile

Expert

- Business development approach more about responding to established demand than creating demand
- Focuses on opportunity/client fit
- Looks for clients with clear needs that match their own capabilities
- Prioritizes clients with budget

To make sure they are seen by clients who are shopping for specific expertise, Experts spend disproportionate time burnishing their images as thought leaders in the market through writing, publishing, speaking, and serving on industry panels and boards. "I speak at roughly fifteen to twenty events per year," one Expert told us. "I don't think the events themselves drive business opportunities, but they increase my brand profile. I'm then a recognizable name whether they attended the event or not. These are events I probably wouldn't go to if I wasn't speaking." And, while Experts certainly want to be *liked* by their clients, they put a much higher premium on being *respected* for their subject matter expertise. As another Expert reported, "My buyers couldn't care less about hanging out with me after work. They call me because they want the smartest person in this field to help them."

Experts are typically responding to inbound demand where clients have a need that matches the Expert's skill set and already have budget set aside for the work. Of course, by the time a client recognizes that it needs outside support and reaches out to the Expert to begin a conversation about hiring them, that client is almost always engaged in simultaneous conversations with other professionals and firms that claim to be experts in the same domains. As a result, Experts end up getting pulled into a lot of competitive pursuits and RFP responses. And because they get relatively few chances compared with other professionals, these pursuits end up creating a fire drill for the rest of the organization, especially a firm's business development team: the Expert will demand countless iterations of pitch decks only to end up not using any of the content. In many firms, the only way Experts hit their growth targets is by receiving partial credit for support they provide on their colleagues' engagements.

One Expert we interviewed summarized this business development approach well: "I don't proactively send a bunch of stuff to clients. They already have the opportunity to receive content from my firm if they want to sign up for our mailing list. I'm also not spending a lot of time with folks checking in to see what they need. We have some dedicated business developers who tend to do more of those 'stay-in-touch' communications. I find that if the client wants to talk to me about something, they will ask." One CEO of a global talent advisory firm put it bluntly when assessing his partners' business development effectiveness: "We have a lot of Experts around here. They like to aggressively wait for the phone to ring."

The Confidant

Our second profile is the Confidant. A Confidant is best described as an old-school trusted advisor. They tend to focus on a small handful of clients and predicate their business development approach on being extremely client-centric (see figure 1-4).

Confidants are highly responsive to client needs and focus on building a reputation for executing high-quality work. As one Confidant explained, a key to his client engagement approach is to provide an experience that exceeds the client's expectations:

> I win when my clients feel like they are getting more than what they pay for. . . . I want every client to feel like they're the most important client to me. I grew up in the restaurant business. . . . If a customer walks in, and the food is great and the service is good . . . they had a pretty good experience; but if the food is

FIGURE 1-4

The Confidant profile

Confidant

- Highly responsive to client needs
- Delivers exceptional client service
- Builds deep relationships with clients
- Leverages strong track record and relationships to get new work
- Emphasizes senior-most relationships

good and the manager or the owner treated them like a VIP, they feel a personal connection. We're in a service industry. If you make that a VIP experience where they feel like that, the likelihood of them wanting to come back is so much higher.

Confidants resist the urge to prescribe solutions to clients and instead tend to rely on their ability to diagnose client needs. One Confidant told us, "I really focus on building a rapport with someone early on, looking for ways to find something in common to talk about so that they trust you and find you credible because you make them feel comfortable. Once that's established, it's about closely listening to what they tell you their problems are." Another declared, "Earning trust isn't about winning work. It's about understanding and scoping what this client actually wants. What are they looking for? Winning work and building and maintaining relationships are different things."

Over time, Confidants develop deep relationships with their clients—especially with senior-most executives and key decision-makers. These relationships begin to transcend business and cross into the personal domain (to the extent that their clients were not already friends; for example, law school or business school classmates). Confidants we interviewed prided themselves on the fact that their closest clients enjoyed spending time with them outside of work. One law firm partner told us that his family regularly goes skiing with the family of her largest client. A senior partner in an executive search firm said that he was the first person his client called with the terrible news that his spouse had unexpectedly passed away. And yet another Confidant told us that the secret to his business development success was as simple as "staying close to [his] friends and then turning forty."

Because of how much Confidants have invested in building these relationships, they tend to be quite protective of them internally. The last thing a Confidant will do is put their carefully developed relationship into the hands of somebody who can't be trusted to handle it with the same care and attention that they themselves have given to it. Not surprisingly, then, they tend not to put any notes in their firm's customer relationship management (CRM) system or otherwise share information about their clients with colleagues. And they can become quite upset if a colleague engages one of their clients without first seeking permission. "I know these people all too well," said the CBDO of an Am Law 50 firm, "They're the ones who call me every month to ask why their biggest client received a copy of the firm newsletter without their permission."

The Confidant's business development mindset is that, because they've delivered such great work, provided such responsive service, and built such strong relationships, they have effectively built a moat around their clients—one that makes it difficult, if not impossible, for a competitor to come in and steal the business. Confidants readily acknowledge the sea change in client buying behavior going on in the professional services market but, in the same breath, seem to think they're immune to the impact of those changes or, at the very least, that they will still be the first professional to get the call from a client when the client has a new need.

One Confidant attributed this to the depth and quality of their client relationships she'd built over the years: "It's definitely gotten more competitive out there. But, at the end of the day, clients always come back to the professionals who've been by their sides." Another explained that "Being an advisor who is trusted with what we do is very rare. And once you've earned that, it's very hard for a competitor to try to muscle out or elbow out a professional who has a position of trust and competence."

For others, a client's loyalty is simply a function of the fact that being disloyal is harder for a client. In the words of one lawyer, "Changing professionals is something people do unwillingly. There's a comfort factor, a laziness factor. People like to take the path of least resistance." Whatever the reason, the consistent refrain we heard from Confidants is that their best client relationships are as safe as they've ever been.

The Debater

Debaters would be uncharitably described by their colleagues as "sharp-elbowed, opinionated know-it-alls." They are highly confident in their

FIGURE 1-5

The Debater profile

Debater

- Always has a different view of the world
- Loves to debate the client on what's best for their business
- Leads with their deep subject matter expertise
- Brings innovative solutions to the client
- Wants the client to follow their lead

subject matter expertise and look for opportunities to reframe clients' understanding of what they need. In this way, they look to create white space between themselves and their competitors (see figure 1-5).

We found that Debaters were most prevalent in spaces in which there was little differentiation between service providers, and rates tended to be more commoditized. As one such partner in an investment banking firm explained to us, "I know that I'm often competing against the other big banks for any meaningful piece of M&A advisory work. We all have great credentials, offer very similar services, and charge roughly the same fees. So if I want to stand apart from the crowd, I need to find an opportunity to disrupt the client's thinking. I lose my fair share of deals, but when I win it's usually because I've brought an innovative, 'outside-the-box' perspective to the client." Another put it more simply: "I'm not really interested in asking clients what they need. They don't really know themselves, so I see it as my job to tell my clients what they need."

As we'll discuss shortly, Debaters don't do particularly well in professional services. Clients were clear that they expect the firms and professionals they work with to challenge them and push their thinking. But it can be mentally exhausting if *every* time they sit down with their professional, they're told, "You're doing it wrong." As one client said, "You don't have to always be a contrarian to earn my respect. Sometimes I just need you to do what I already know needs to be done."

Previous research has found that this profile is the winning approach in B2B sales. That Debaters fall short in professional services was particularly surprising to us. A Debater approach can work when you're selling a product—like software or medical devices—but when you *are* the product, the approach falls short. As a business largely founded on relationships, professionals need to tread carefully between pushing the client's thinking and pushing the client away.

The Realist

Next, we have the Realist. These professionals are completely transparent about what they can and can't deliver, what an engagement or matter will cost, and what the client should realistically expect in terms of outcomes and value (see figure 1-6). They look to avoid putting themselves, their teams, or their firms in no-win situations. For example, they avoid engagements that are unlikely to deliver their intended outcomes or work that can't be delivered on time or on budget.

This isn't to suggest that firms don't want every professional to be truthful and transparent with their clients. They do. But what makes Realists unique is that this is the crux of their business development approach. Why? Because Realists know that every client out there has been burned in the past by a professional who has overstated their experience and capabilities, left them holding the bag on a poorly implemented solution, or sent a surprise invoice after the conclusion of an engagement that was well in excess of the client's stated budget. So they look to set themselves in the market by doing the exact opposite.

FIGURE 1-6

The Realist profile

Realist

- Focuses on setting proper expectations with the client
- Openly discusses budget, fees, and other money-related issues with clients
- Comfortable telling the client no
- Shields themselves from no-win client situations

Realists can be brutally honest with their clients. One Realist we interviewed told us "Price is a big factor for our clients. We try to be open with them about what the work will require, give them a range of hours, and so forth. Sometimes clients tell us, 'Well, this is what it took last year' or 'Another firm said it will take half of the number of hours you're proposing.' When that happens, we tell them we can't match it." Asked why her clients are loyal to her, one consultant we spoke to said simply, "Because I always do what I say I'm going to do, in a time frame that's reasonable for them, and at or under the budget they set aside for the work." Realists double major in the "trust" part of the "trusted advisor" concept.

Interestingly, while we do see that the best B2B salespeople use honesty and transparency to instill customer confidence and avoid customer indecision, we don't see a similar Realist profile in the B2B sales space. This likely has to do with the fact that B2B salespeople, for the most part, sell tangible products to customers—products that customers can touch and feel for themselves. B2B buyers regularly engage in demos, pilots, and proof-of-concept trials for the products they're considering purchasing—all of which enable them to verify whether the salesperson's claims about capabilities, performance, and projected return on investment are accurate.

But professional services require a different type of sale. Regardless of whether a client is hiring a lawyer, banker, accountant, or consultant, they are buying something intangible: a professional's advisory skills. As Clay Christensen, Dina Wang, and Derek van Bever argued in a 2013 *Harvard Business Review* article,

> Like most other professional services, consulting is highly opaque compared with manufacturing-based companies. The most prestigious firms have evolved into "solution shops" whose recommendations are created in the black box of the team room. It's incredibly difficult for clients to judge a consultancy's performance in advance, because they are usually hiring the firm for specialized knowledge and capability that they themselves lack.

It's even hard to judge after a project has been completed, because so many external factors, including quality of execution, management transition, and the passage of time, influence the outcome of the consultants' recommendations.[3]

It is for this reason that most professionals go to such lengths to demonstrate their credentials when they pitch for new business—pointing to similar clients for whom they've done comparable work in the past in order to allay any concerns the prospective client may have about selecting them. The simple fact that buying professional services is ultimately a black-box purchase helps explain why we find Realists among our five professional profiles.

The Activator

Our final profile is the Activator. Activators are super-connectors. Their professional network is arguably their most important strategic asset. It's the platform they use to build their books of business and is, therefore, an asset that they purposefully build, cultivate, and nurture (see the profile in figure 1-7).

Not surprisingly, Activators are heavy users of platforms like LinkedIn—regularly posting, commenting, liking, and connecting. But their network building extends to live settings like firm-sponsored events and industry conferences as well. These are the professionals who don't

FIGURE 1-7

The Activator profile

Activator

- Leverages events and social platforms to build a robust client network
- Educates clients on emerging trends and issues
- Proactively engages clients on new opportunities to work together
- Makes introductions to other partners and practice areas

attend an event *hoping* business development will happen, but who attend events to *make* business development happen. Before an event, they will scour the list of registrants to identify individuals they want to connect with. They go to the event with a goal of making a certain number of new connections or having a certain number of client conversations. They set up breakfasts, lunches, coffees, and dinners to establish new connections and nurture existing ones. They are then diligent about recording, tracking, and following up with their connections once they return to the office.

Our research team debated whether "Connector" was a better name than "Activator" for this profile, but ultimately concluded that connection was only part of the story. In interviews, Activators were very clear that while network building is absolutely necessary, it is also insufficient as a business development approach. For an Activator, a robust professional network represents potential, not kinetic, energy. It needs to be *activated* to result in paid work.

The most intriguing part of the Activator story is how they convert connections into conversations and then convert conversations into paying client relationships. They do this by proactively engaging their connections with new ideas—new ways to make money, save money, or mitigate risk—ideas that clients themselves may have missed, overlooked, or just not had sufficient time to explore on their own. In this respect, they are the opposite of the Expert. Rather than waiting for the phone to ring or responding to a need the client already knows they have, Activators proactively alert clients to needs they often don't know they have. "I know how busy my clients are," explained one Activator, "They rely on me to monitor the landscape for them and alert them to new threats and opportunities."

To a person, Activators explained that much of this proactive outreach is done off the clock—in other words, they look to deliver some initial advice and guidance to the client to earn some goodwill and give the client a chance to kick the tires a bit on their advisory skills, but they aren't looking to bill the client for the time. An investment banker we interviewed told us that he will regularly engage prospective clients with new ideas and offer to hop on a call or grab a coffee to discuss them. "Even if the client ends up bidding out the work," she explained, "I'd much rather be in a position where I'm the person who brought the idea to them and shaped their understanding of the opportunity. This puts me at a distinct advantage, even in a competitive pursuit situation."

A final point about the Activator: unlike the Confidant, who tends to hoard client relationships internally, Activators proactively bring their colleagues into their client relationships—they are constantly looking for ways in which other professionals or practice areas in their firms can deliver value for a client. They consider themselves more "general contractors for expertise" than the sole source of expertise. Sometimes, an Activator will find that nobody in their firm can help a client with a particular need, but this doesn't deter them from trying to connect the client with somebody in their network they feel can provide value.

Profile Distribution across Segments

Before we look at how these different professionals compare with one another in terms of performance, let's first look at how they distribute across the professional services industry (see figure 1-8).

To compare profile prevalence, we let the data place each respondent into the profile they major in. As discussed earlier, each professional has elements of all five profiles, but at the same time, each individual spikes in one.

When we look at representation of these profiles across the professional services industry, we find that it's fairly evenly distributed. There's a bit of a deficit in the Debater profile at 17 percent. This is unsurprising given our discussion about how a Debater approach can be a tough pill for clients to swallow. The remaining profiles sit between 20 percent to 22 percent of the overall sample. In other words, there's no single, dominant approach.

Clicking a level deeper, we find that there are interesting variations across the different subverticals. For instance, there's a pronounced spike

FIGURE 1-8

Profile distribution

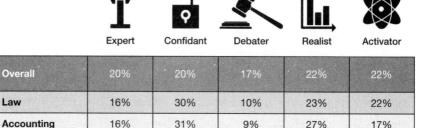

	Expert	Confidant	Debater	Realist	Activator
Overall	20%	20%	17%	22%	22%
Law	16%	30%	10%	23%	22%
Accounting	16%	31%	9%	27%	17%
Consulting	17%	7%	18%	33%	25%
Investment banking	18%	9%	37%	7%	30%
Talent advisory	20%	16%	17%	18%	30%
Public relations/ communications	40%	3%	22%	23%	12%

in Confidants, at more than 30 percent of the professionals in law and accounting. When we show this to firm leaders, they aren't surprised. Most point to the fact that the "trusted advisor" approach to building a book of business has been preached for decades in these industries.

Consulting, on the other hand, spikes in Realists—which is perhaps a function of the fact that consultants struggle more with instilling confidence in clients that their engagements will deliver the projected impact. Numerous C-level executives we spoke with lamented the amount of money they've poured into expensive transformation engagements—often spending upward of seven figures with consultants to support these initiatives—only to feel like they were left holding the bag without results to show for their investments.

In PR and communications, 40 percent of professionals are Experts, which is likely a reflection of the fact that in many PR firms (and particularly in those we studied), professionals often cut their teeth not in PR but on the client side—or perhaps in government or journalism—and were explicitly hired for their deep subject matter expertise.

Investment banking has a surplus of Debaters, which makes sense considering that the advisory fees most banks charge are fairly consistent across the industry and that, when selecting an investment banker, clients will often go through a formal selection and bid process. As one client said, "You need to like your banker, but you need to love your deal." This leads to a more competitive dynamic, which creates more of a "sales" feel to the industry than what you might find in other segments.

The only segment in which we find Activators to be the dominant profile is in executive search and talent advisory. Again, this stands to reason given the importance of networking in that business. For a professional in one of these firms, their networks really *are* treated as a strategic business asset.

Performance Analysis

The fact that there are five unique data-based professional profiles is in itself revealing. This is especially true for firm leaders who spend a massive amount of time thinking about the makeup of the broader organization as well as the composition of different practices, regions, and offices—and how all of this affects firm performance.

Professionals and firm leaders have long lacked an actionable framework to think about the approaches different professionals take to engage clients and develop relationships. Because professional services roles are fundamentally different from sales roles, traditional sales methodologies—no matter how well researched—often fail to be adopted. And those frameworks that do exist for professional services are either too generic or not based on real data, which again leads professionals to reject them, if not to feel dejected by them, as they find these approaches to be of little help in a changing client buying environment.

But as valuable as it is to know that there are five unique paths professionals choose when it comes to their business development efforts, it's much more valuable for professionals to understand which of these paths

FIGURE 1-9

Performance distribution by professional profile

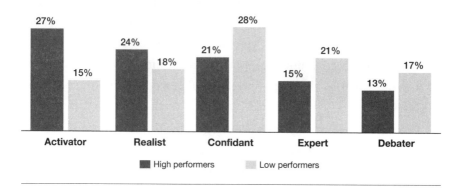

High performers   *Low performers*

to embrace and which to avoid as the data clearly show that they are not all created equal when it comes to performance impact.

To assess the impact of the five profiles on business development performance, we ran two types of analysis. First, we ran a descriptive analysis, placing every professional into the profile they major in and then overlaying the performance ratings their firms provided to see which profiles tended to have the greatest number of high performers and which had the greatest number of low performers. (The results are shown in figure 1-9.)

When we compare the performance of professionals in each of these profiles, we see that Activators represent the biggest proportion of the high-performer population, comprising 27 percent of this group. Realists finish second at 24 percent, and the percentages trail off from there, with Confidants at 21 percent, Experts at 15 percent, and Debaters at 13 percent. But what really clarifies the performance picture is when we overlay the low-performer population on top of the profiles. Doing this reveals that Activators really do dominate the performance landscape— not only are they the largest percentage of the high-performer population, but they're the smallest percentage of the low-performer population. In fact, only 15 percent of professionals who major in an Activator approach fall into the low-performer category.

Readers may wonder about the efficacy of a Realist approach since those who spike in this approach finished a close second to Activators from a high-performance standpoint. But the effectiveness of a Realist approach is muted by the fact that 18 percent of Realists—nearly one-fifth—also fall into the low-performer population. So, unlike Activators, there is only a marginal difference between the number of high-performing Realists and low-performing Realists. For Confidants, Experts, and Debaters, the story is much worse. The data shows that a professional pursuing any of these approaches is much more likely to be a low performer than a high performer—a finding that shocks many firm leaders, especially when they realize how many of their professionals actually fall into these categories.

Still, while the odds of being a high performer are greatest for professionals who major in the Activator approach, the data also shows that one could be a high performer pursuing *any* of the five approaches. This is where predictive analysis is critical. A descriptive analysis is useful to understand what has already happened. But only a predictive analysis like regression can show us what is most likely to happen in the future. What would happen, in other words, if a professional chose one of these five different paths as a way to improve their performance? (See the appendix for more on comparing descriptive and predictive results.)

To understand the regression output, readers should think about the relationship between profile strength and performance. Profile strength measures the degree to which a professional is demonstrating the attributes associated with a given profile—from weak to strong. And then, in terms of performance, we're talking about a professional's individual revenue generation.

Let's look at what happens when a fiftieth-percentile performer chooses to double down on the skills associated with any one of the profiles. For instance, what would happen to their performance if they went from being a weak Confidant to a strong Confidant or a weak Realist to a strong Realist?

The results are eye-opening. It turns out that four of the five profiles—Realists, Debaters, Confidants, and Experts—are, in fact, *negatively*

FIGURE 1-10

How the profiles affect performance

This chart illustrates the effect on revenue when the average-performing partner leans harder into a particular profile. Moving from a weak to a strong demonstration of Activator skills would result in a revenue-generation increase of up to 32 percent. The opposite is true for the other approaches, all of which are negatively correlated with performance. For example, a shift from weak to strong in the Expert profile would result in a drop in revenue generation of up to 15%.

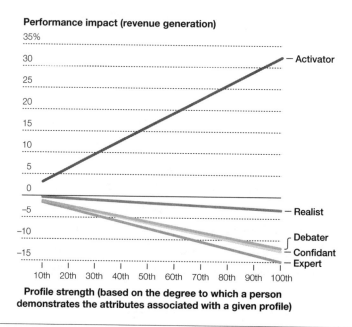

correlated with performance (see figure 1-10). The more this average professional were to lean into any of those approaches, the worse they would perform relative to how much revenue they could generate. More concerning than this, however, is that 78 percent of the professionals we studied fell into one of those four profiles.

These professionals are not knowingly selecting a business development approach they believe will make them less effective. Rather, for one reason or another—whether it's guidance they've been given by their mentors or leaders or the way in which their incentive structure motivates them to operate—they have chosen a business development path that won't lead them to high performance. Leaders looking for an explanation as to why their firm's growth hasn't met expectations—or perhaps why it hasn't grown at all—need look no further than this finding. When nearly 80 percent of professionals are locked into a counterproductive approach to finding, engaging, and growing client relationships, growth stalls are to be expected.

But while these four profiles showed a negative correlation with performance—the opposite was true of the Activator. This approach was the only one of the five that showed a positive correlation with revenue generation. And the relationship wasn't simply positive, it was overwhelmingly so. If the average professional were to move from weak to strong on their demonstration of Activator skills, they could improve their personal revenue generation by up to 32 percent. This is a huge number for an individual professional, let alone for a firm leader, considering the impact of an Activator approach across a practice, office, region, or entire organization. Put simply, there are no other investments leaders can make that can create this sort of performance lift.

What's also amazing about the performance impact of the Activator approach is that it is positive in a linear way. Every incremental gain in Activator skills yields a proportionate return in revenue generation. This "gearing effect" is a powerful finding for professionals to consider since it tells them that there is no minimum required baseline before a focus on Activator behaviors pays off. A professional at the zero percentile will see performance gains with *any* improvement in their Activator skills. And a professional who has a typical baseline level of Activator skills can continue to ratchet up their performance by getting incrementally better. Even world-class Activators performing at the ninetieth percentile of skill demonstration can still make positive gains by closing their few remaining gaps. Performance gains do not tail off or flatten at any point on the Activator journey.

For firm leaders, these findings tell us that selecting a business development approach shouldn't be a "choose your own adventure" for professionals. Instead, there is clearly one approach—the Activator approach—that should be the standard for professionals to aspire to.

The Activator Model

By this point, readers are likely wondering: Can I learn to become an Activator?

Fortunately, the answer is yes. And we're going to spend the rest of this book teaching you the ins and outs of the Activator approach—the critical moving parts, the data and scientific underpinnings to them, and practical guidance for professionals to start developing their own Activator motion with current and prospective clients out in the market.

In addition to the quantitative research we've shared already, our team at DCMi has conducted hundreds of hours of structured behavioral interviews with partners, including a significant number of Activators. In addition, we've now trained thousands of fee-earners across all levels of professional services firms, from junior associates to senior partners, practice leaders, and management committee members. We've concluded that there is a set of distinct behaviors Activators demonstrate, habits that underpin their day-to-day business development efforts, and mindsets that Activators possess. These all come together in a discrete set of pivot points or moments in the client relationship when Activators seek to distinguish and differentiate themselves. Together, these attributes comprise what we call the Activator model, as summarized in figure 1-11.

Taken as a whole, the Activator model is the decoder ring to the winning client engagement approach. Importantly, the Activator model is *not* a sales methodology. Those frameworks tend to be based on linear processes that require sellers to adhere to each prescribed step in the sequence, similar to how one would bake a cake. The Activator model isn't a step-by-step process in this way. Instead, it's a road map for any professional who is looking to develop more of an Activator element to their own business development efforts; it can be adopted wholesale or in parts, depending on where a partner spots opportunities to improve their own personal approach. For instance, one partner might see a need to bring more regularity and consistency to their business development

FIGURE 1-11

The Activator model

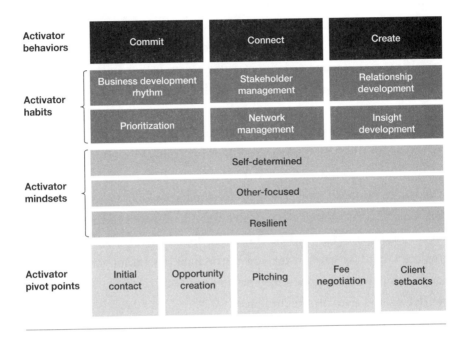

efforts, so they may focus on committing habits such as business development rhythm and prioritization, whereas another partner may
feel that their opportunity for improvement is in pitching or dealing
with client setbacks. There is no starting or ending point in the Activator model—no right or wrong way to begin one's journey to greater
Activator-ness.

In the following chapters, we will expand on these concepts and paint
the full picture of Activator habits, behaviors, and mindsets.

Should every professional be an Activator?

Before we dig into the elements of the Activator model, it's worth paus-
ing to address the most common question we get from professionals and
firm leaders when they are first introduced to the Activator research:
Should every professional be an Activator?

The answer to this question is more complicated than it might seem, and it really depends on one's vantage point. First, there are the professionals who have been successful in their careers pursuing a different path. Years as a Confidant may have built strong relationships that have generated enough business to sustain them. Or years as a deep Expert in specific terrain areas has led to regular referrals. For those professionals, a wholesale change in approach at this stage in their careers would not make sense. As such, our guidance is moderated: keep doing what has made you successful. In other words, if it ain't broke, don't fix it. But at the same time, recognize the client buying environment is rapidly changing—so, "what got you here won't get you there," as Marshall Goldsmith famously said. These professionals should look to add Activator tools to their toolbelts and evolve their approaches to better suit the needs of a changing market. Our recommendation therefore is not to *replace* what has worked for you in the past but rather to *enrich* your current business development approach—and future proof your success—with targeted Activator techniques.

On the other hand, you may be a fee-earner struggling with business development who is looking for a new approach. Or maybe you once had a consistent growing book of business but find that is no longer the case. If this is you, then becoming an Activator may represent the sort of hard reset you're looking for. Or perhaps you're an associate just starting to think about shaping your own business development approach as you track toward partner or as you look to move from the corporate or government world into private practice. If this is you, we recommend committing to an Activator approach now—better to develop the right habits early in your tenure as a professional rather than having to undo bad ones later.

Regardless of one's starting point, however, a simple point bears repeating here: because there is a straight, linear relationship between Activator profile strength and business development performance, *every incremental improvement* in one's Activator-ness will yield improvements in business development effectiveness. So, the idea of becoming an Activator is actually somewhat misplaced, in part because it's not necessary to completely adopt an Activator approach to see benefit from Activator techniques. And more to the point, the idea of dramatically changing one's approach can feel daunting and unattainable, thereby increasing the odds that fee-earners abandon the journey before it even begins.

Some professionals, aside from their own interest in developing Activator skills, may wonder how Activator-ness applies to client-facing teams that they may be a part of. Specifically, do all members of a client team need to be Activators? Most professionals in the market today find that they are engaging their clients in more of a team-based fashion as clients demand more holistic solutions to their increasingly complex issues. Realistically, it's unlikely that an entire client team would end up being composed of pure Activators. Instead, it's likely to include a host of professionals with different levels of Activator capability. This is perfectly normal and, in fact, a good thing. Most client-facing teams benefit from a diversity of skills and strengths. A great client-facing team will include Experts who have renowned, market-leading capabilities, Confidants who can build deep client relationships and smooth over any issues, Realists who can manage client expectations, even Debaters who can push the client's thinking when needed. Still, as a practical point, we recommend that the professional who is running point on the team and acting as the primary commercial interface to the client have strong Activator skills.

Summary

While there has been a significant amount of research done on the approaches used by B2B sales professionals, there has been a relative dearth of research on "doer-sellers" in professional services firms—a role that is fundamentally different from that of a salesperson.

Our analysis revealed that each professional falls into one of five statistically defined business development profiles or approaches: Experts, Confidants, Debaters, Realists, and Activators. While each professional typically possesses a combination of the attributes associated with all of the five profiles, it's also true that each spikes in one of the five as their primary business development approach.

Experts are reactive business developers who lean heavily on their public reputations as accomplished subject matter experts to attract clients to reach out to them for the services they can provide. Confidants are old-school trusted advisors who focus on building competitive moats around their key clients by forging deep relationships predicated on their highly responsive service and exceptional work product. Debaters are highly opinionated professionals who seek to reframe the client's own understanding of their needs in a way that creates white space between themselves and other professionals competing for the client's business. Realists are truthful, transparent, honest brokers with their clients—a posture that they believe helps instill confidence with the typical client, who has likely been burned in the past by professionals or firms that have overpromised and underdelivered. Finally, Activators are super-connectors who invest heavily in building and nurturing their professional networks and then converting their network connections into paying client relationships. They do this by proactively bringing new ideas to their clients about new ways to make money, save money, or mitigate risk.

While there are many ways a professional could become a high-performing business developer, the data is very clear that in today's far more challenging client buying environment, there is one approach that is disproportionately more likely to lead to successful commercial outcomes: becoming an Activator. The message to firm leaders is equally clear: figuring out how to build a book of business shouldn't be a "choose your own adventure" for associates or partners. Firms should encourage their client-facing professionals to develop Activator skills and should use every tool available—from training to enablement to incentives, rewards, and recognition—to nudge their professionals onto an Activator path.

— 2 —

How Activators Commit to Business Development

Katie Vickery, a partner at the UK law firm Osborne Clarke, has a commitment to her business development routine that has paid off handsomely. She posts on LinkedIn, likes or comments on others' posts, and keeps track of role changes and personal events. She reads as much as possible, scanning the news in search of valuable updates that she can send to clients. She also creates thought leadership videos: when inspiration strikes, she goes into Osborne Clarke's in-house studio, records a video in about twenty minutes, and posts it on LinkedIn. Her process nets her roughly one new business opportunity every two to three days.[1]

Adam Ludwiczak, a partner at Marathon Capital, a financial services firm with a focus on renewable energy projects, told us that he maps out his business development activities before the workweek begins. Every Sunday night, he writes three categories on a blank sheet of paper: client interactions, deal-specific action items, and ways to engage prospects and clients. As he plans the week's business development time, he uses that framework as a guide for whom to reach out to and for what reason.

At the end of each day, he emails notes to his direct reports, who feed them into their CRM system. He tags relevant parties on opportunities so that team members can work together to keep the business development pipeline moving.[2]

Jessica Stallmeyer is the financial services industry lead at the consultancy Guidehouse. Her team is focused on serving the needs of the largest, most complex financial institutions in the world—something that requires constant commitment and coordination. To help track business development activities, they maintain a custom dashboard that is visible to all team members. It tracks all interactions with a client at every level of the client organization—from ongoing engagements to work they are currently pitching, early-stage conversations that might yield paid work down the road, and even nonbillable work (e.g., sending relevant thought leadership to key contacts) that is helping to reinforce Guidehouse's value to the client. "The dashboard helps us stay coordinated but also creates a culture of mutual accountability to business development. The market is way too competitive for there to be any letup in our client engagement efforts. The moment we take our foot off the gas, competitors will swoop in to fill the void."

These professionals are demonstrating the first pillar of an Activator approach: committing to business development. Across this chapter, we'll unpack this behavior more fully and provide a road map for any professional to follow in order to add this critical dimension to their own business development approach.

What It Means (and Doesn't Mean) to Have a Commitment to Business Development

Because professionals are responsible for selling and delivering the work, business development easily gets crowded out by other tasks—especially when those professionals feel they don't have a natural affinity for business development. And when business development skills aren't maintained, they start to atrophy.

This doesn't happen to Activators. Unlike most professionals, Activators see business development as a core part of their job that needs to be protected in the same way as any other responsibility, including executing client work. They were the only one of the five profiles we studied that carved out and protected time for business development. Nearly 90 percent of Activators report that they reserve time for this every week. For non-Activators, business development is a side-of-the-desk activity—something they do in their spare time, when they are not busy with client work—and only 36 percent of them report that they reserve time for it every week. But for an Activator, business development is like going to the gym—it's a regular routine that they adhere to. If they don't get to it in the morning, they do it in the afternoon, and if the afternoon gets crowded, they do it in the evening.

Activators are far less prone to the frenetic business development patterns exhibited by their peers. The amount of business development time they spend per week tends to be smooth, predictable, and consistent. Non-Activators show more of a propensity for long periods when no business development takes place punctuated by episodic spikes in commercial activity normally associated with responding to urgent client needs or RFPs. For an Activator, engaging clients and pitching for business are always-on processes, not events.

Not only do Activators demonstrate a more consistent routine of business development, they also show a level of patience and persistence we didn't find with other professionals. In our interviews, Activators told us that while they are quick to disqualify bad-fit client opportunities, they are also willing to invest significant time—not just months but sometimes years—developing relationships with good-fit clients, even when those clients initially show little desire to engage commercially. For instance, only 8 percent of non-Activators reported that they would be willing to pursue an unresponsive client for two to three years, while nearly 20 percent of Activators said they would readily do so.

A commitment to business development is critical in today's challenging client buying environment. Why? Because it naturally translates into having a bigger pipeline of client opportunities. They are there as insurance should a professional's existing client sever ties and take their business elsewhere—something we know is far more likely to happen today than in the past.

This commitment to business development enables Activators to engage clients with greater regularity, helping to ward off the "relationship decay" that can naturally set in when professionals aren't actively connected with clients. In other words, it helps them to stay top-of-mind with clients even when not performing paid work for them. Eighty-two percent of Activators believe it is necessary to be in contact with clients at least once per month to maintain their relationship. Only 62 percent of non-Activators report this level of ongoing commitment to client relationship maintenance.

Activators never see a client relationship as "safe." Overall, our respondents said that 56 percent of the business they generate is competitive, but Activators assume that percentage to be much higher. For instance, Activators in the consulting world said 63 percent of their business is competitive, while Activators in investment banking estimated this figure at 71 percent. One Activator told us he learned early in his career that "you're always better off assuming you won't have a client for more than a few years. If you operate under the assumption that even your best clients will leave you at some point, you work hard to build a pipeline of future clients that can replenish your book of business." This mentality creates a strong hedge against client churn. Another Activator said, "Infrequent engagement isn't just bad for me as a business developer, it's bad for my clients. There's a lot of value in them knowing I'm actively out in the market, looking for threats and opportunities on their behalf. If I go radio silent, what evidence would they have that I'm looking out for them?"

Skeptics might assume that Activators are sales-focused professionals who massively overweight their time toward revenue generation, handing off execution work to other team members. But they'd be wrong. Activators do spend 37 percent more time on business development than non-Activators, but they don't spend *most* of their time on it.

In fact, we found something surprising when we looked into the time-tracking data collected by their firms: the amount of time they self-report spending on business development tends to be much higher than the amount they record in their firms' time-tracking tools. When we dug into this discrepancy, we learned two things. First, Activators tend to "double-count" client-facing time in their minds. They consider many client-facing interactions, even if tracked as billable time or project time, as serving the additional purpose of business development. One Activator we interviewed claimed that she spent 100 percent of her time on business development—a purposeful exaggeration to drive home the point that *any* client-facing time should be considered business development time. Second, Activators tended to report to us that they used "found" or "repurposed" time for business development. For instance, some told us they used their morning dog-walking time to engage clients on LinkedIn or used their morning train commute to send emails to target clients—none of which ends up being reported in the time-tracking tool.

Another incorrect assumption is that Activators spend far more time on new client acquisition than developing and growing existing client relationships. We found that Activators balance these two types of business development almost evenly. They spend slightly more time on existing clients (23 percent) than pursuing net new clients (22 percent). In contrast, non-Activators dramatically overweight their business development time toward existing clients, which is consistent with the conventional belief that performing good work for a client will automatically lead to the next piece of business. We found that they spend 37 percent of their business development time on existing clients and 17 percent on new ones.

Committing Like an Activator

There are two habits central to an Activator's commitment to business development: rhythm and prioritization. These habits are all about creating (and protecting) the business development cadence that characterizes an Activator's go-to-market approach.

Habit 1: Business development rhythm

What does it mean to have an Activator-like business development rhythm? Activators see client development and relationship building as an ongoing habit that requires practical and emotional consistency, week by week and month by month. *Business development rhythm* refers to the idea that Activators have figured out how to make business development a regular habit.

From our quantitative research, we know that Activators:

- Don't allow business development time to be crowded out by client work or other responsibilities

- Reserve time to conduct business development every week

- Consistently engage clients

- Rigorously follow up on opportunities that have been discussed

- Track contacts and follow-ups in the firm's CRM system

Developing a consistent, metronomic cadence. The consistency with which Activators reserve time for business development is the most critical, practical difference between Activators and non-Activators. It's easy to push business development activities to the background and return to them when client work slows. "Business development is what I do when I'm not working with clients" is a phrase we heard often from Confidants or Experts. Indeed, this can appear as a very client-centric perspective. But when professionals adopt this mindset, it translates into far greater reliance on existing clients than on new business. In today's unpredictable client buying environment, that's a risky strategy.

Avoiding intermittent business development. There are three major problems with inconsistent business development. The lack of new contacts is the most obvious and fundamental. Business development is, at its heart, a numbers game, and it takes a certain number of new contacts in any industry to generate a new lead or opportunity.

The second problem with intermittent business development is that it leads to opportunity "spoilage." Let's say we've met a new contact, Jamie, at an industry event, and we exchange business cards. We're excited about Jamie because he is at a company we've hoped to work with for years. We follow up with him within a week. We send him an email and a LinkedIn connection message. We share an important insight in both messages that we think he'll appreciate. Jamie may even write back with a signal that he'd be open to working with us in the future. But in the following weeks, a bunch of client deadlines pop up. Before we know it, three months have passed since our last contact with Jamie.

Now what? The awkwardness of any outreach is amplified by the months of silence. Anything we send Jamie is necessarily going to sound a bit more commercial, so we wait until we see news that would naturally prompt us to reach out to him. But a few weeks pass before this happens. Before we know it, it's been six months without contact. By this time, Jamie has forgotten about the initial connection at the event. He's attended other events in the meantime and exchanged another ten business cards. Best case: Jamie appreciates the email, and maybe he has some work for us, but he doesn't feel the relationship is formed enough to trust us with the work, so he takes our insights to the professionals with whom he has worked in the past. If we're lucky, he adds us to the list of providers receiving the RFP. But more likely than not, the email we send him is just another vendor contact he ignores.

This leads us to the third and most devastating problem with inconsistent business development: it's inefficient. New contacts need nurturing. The longer we take between interactions, the more work it requires to rebuild that relationship. That first in-person interaction we have with a prospect or client has a critical role in releasing oxytocin, something referred to by Dr. Paul Zak and other researchers as "the trust molecule."[3] Research has repeatedly shown that frequency of interaction and joint activity are necessary to move relationships from weaker to stronger. The more we communicate with others, the stronger the emotional bond.[4] If we take a start-and-stop approach to relationship development, we must do much more work to get to the same level of trust compared with ongoing or regular contact.

Getting into the habit of business development. Developing a consistent, metronomic cadence to business development is easier said than done, especially for professionals for whom business development doesn't come naturally. It can feel a bit like a New Year's resolution that we'll stick with for a week or two before letting it fall by the wayside. In short, it takes willpower to get a new behavior to stick.

Fortunately, willpower is a skill that can be developed like any other. In the 1960s, researchers at Stanford conducted experiments on self-regulation in kids. In the initial experiment, young children were given the option to get one marshmallow now or wait five minutes and get two. On average, those who waited later averaged 210 points higher on their SATs than the others. While there have been questions about the replicability of these long-term implications, there is no question that delayed gratification is a useful skill.[5] Additional experiments during the 1980s confirmed the finding that willpower and self-motivation are learnable skills.

But how do we make it stick? To improve the odds that our business development rhythm becomes a new habit and not just a flavor of the week, aspiring Activators should heed the guidance of habit-formation experts like James Clear.

In his book *Atomic Habits*, Clear identifies several tactics one can take to improve the odds of success.[6] The first is what he calls "habit timing"—specifically, when during the day or week one devotes time to the new habit.[7] It turns out that there are better and worse times to create a new habit.

A team of Case Western Reserve University psychologists, led by Roy Baumeister, wondered why, if willpower is a learned skill, we do not have the same level of willpower all the time? Some days we have no problem going for a jog in the evening; other days we can't be bothered. In a breakthrough study, Baumeister's team described how subjects were recruited for an experiment around taste perception and were told to skip a meal so that they were hungry when testing began.[8] When they arrived, there were cookies in front of them. The entire room smelled like fresh-baked cookies. But next to the cookies were bowls of radishes. Half of the subjects were given some of those delicious cookies to eat, and the other half were told they could eat only the radishes. Some of the radish eaters were really frustrated—they would smell the cookies and stare at them longingly while sadly eating their radishes. Then the researchers came back into the room, told the subjects to wait fifteen minutes, and then gave them a puzzle to complete. It looked simple, but it was deceivingly challenging. The researchers found that those who were asked to exercise restraint and eat the radishes had already depleted much of their willpower and made far fewer attempts to solve the puzzle—they devoted less than half the time compared with the cookie-eaters. The conclusion of the research: willpower is a finite resource that can be exhausted.

What does this mean for nurturing a business development habit? Practically speaking, if professionals equate business development with "eating their radishes"—something that is good for them but not particularly enjoyable—they should do it early in the day or early in the week before they deplete the willpower required to get it done. Most Activators therefore do early-bird business development. "I am pretty religious about doing some business development while I'm having my first cup of coffee in the kitchen," one Activator said, "I don't allow myself to read the sports pages until I check a few things off my BD list." Another told us that as soon as she takes her seat on the train for her morning commute, she opens her laptop and works through her business development tasks for the thirty minutes it takes her to reach her office.

A related concept is an idea Clear calls "habit stacking," which is when one piggybacks new habits on top of well-ingrained existing ones.[9] Again, consider the above examples of doing business development while having morning coffee or during the morning commute. Those are established habits that have already "stuck," so the idea of habit-stacking is to now marry a new habit—in this case, client engagement—to an older, established one. Habit stacking works because of a neurological phenomenon called "synaptic pruning," which is the natural process by which the connections between neurons in our brains, called "synapses," are either pruned or reinforced depending on what we choose to focus on. The more you do something, the stronger the synapses become, and the less you do something, the weaker they are. This is why we get better at things the more we practice (i.e., "practice makes perfect"). Clear explains that once we've stacked a new habit on top of an old one, we can then build "habit chains."[10] For example, you might start building a business development rhythm by attaching it to an existing habit (e.g., "While I'm on the treadmill in the morning, I'll compose a voice memo to myself with my BD punch list for the day"). Then, once this habit is ingrained, you can attach a new one (e.g., "As soon as I get back from my workout, I'll block thirty minutes on my calendar during the day to get after the items on the list I created") and so on (e.g., "As soon as my thirty-minute BD time block time begins, I will start working through my list of items and check them off as I complete them").

Another tactic Clear highlights is "habit location," or *where* specifically we choose to perform a new habit.[11] Existing locations tend to already have habits and routines associated with them, so a good idea is to try changing locations to develop new habits. One Activator told us that she does her business development in a coffee shop around the corner from her firm's offices. "I associate my office with doing client work," she explained. "I found that I had a hard time switching gears to business development while sitting in that location. I make much more progress with a simple change of scenery. That coffee shop has become my business development headquarters."

Finding "habit partners" can also be an effective way to reinforce new behaviors. This is when we surround ourselves with people who possess the habits we want to develop in ourselves.[12] Clear points to a study that found that your risk of developing obesity increases by nearly 60 percent when your friends are obese (even when those friends don't live nearby and with whom physical interaction is infrequent).[13] This is why people often find it more effective to stick to an exercise routine when they're part of a group, like a CrossFit gym or running club. It's also the glue behind popular exercise-oriented social networking apps like Strava.

Above all else, however, experts like Clear are emphatic that one of the most important things to do when starting a new habit is to make the commitment small, specific, and actionable.[14] Telling yourself, "I'm going to start spending more time on business development every week" is much like saying "I'm going to get in shape" or "I'm going to be a better friend." These well-intentioned ideas are too big, too lofty, and can feel too hard to take on—a recipe for habit abandonment. New habits stick best when they start as small, manageable steps. A commitment like spending fifteen minutes a day on business development, which can then be increased to thirty minutes or forty-five minutes a day over time, is far more likely to stick than a goal that is too big. Instead of "spending fifteen minutes a day on business development," a more-likely-to-be-adopted commitment like "spending fifteen minutes on business development while I have my coffee in the morning at the kitchen table" is the sort of precise and actionable start that future habits are made of.

One final word of guidance: aspiring Activators must remember that developing a commitment to business development won't happen overnight. Readers may be familiar with the oft-repeated guidance that it takes twenty-one days to form a habit. Unfortunately, this is a myth that started with psychologist Dr. Maxwell Maltz in 1960. The plastic surgeon turned psychologist noted a twenty-one-day time frame in which patients got used to their new faces, amputations, and the like. He theorized that this time frame may also be the time it takes to get used to a new home, for example. Somewhere along the line, this was accepted as truth.

The reality is that most habits take longer to form. Psychologist Phillippa Lally and her colleagues asked ninety-six volunteers to commit to a new eating, drinking, or other daily activity for twelve weeks and to record whether they carried out the behavior each day.[15] The length of time depended in part on how complex the activity was, with "drinking more water" taking less time to build as a habit than something like "doing fifty sit-ups a day." In the end, the team found that it actually takes anywhere from 18 to 254 days to build a habit—with the average being 66 days. But the research also shows that once this threshold is crossed, these habits start to become ingrained to the point where *not* doing it every day feels strange.

Habit-formation experts say that developing a "short memory" is critical. Developing a new habit or routine is about patience and consistency, not perfection. If you slip, get back on track quickly and reflect on what caused the slippage and whether you can avoid it moving forward. Setbacks should be expected. The key is to get back into your routine immediately.

Clear recommends that people employ the "Seinfeld Strategy," which comes from comedian Jerry Seinfeld.[16] Seinfeld, who has been celebrated for his longevity as a comedian and entertainer, has explained that one of the secrets to his success is his daily commitment to writing new material. Seinfeld keeps a wall calendar in his office and puts a big red "X" on every day he writes new material, focusing not on whether the material is any good but on whether he can maintain the streak for as long as possible. As Clear explains,

> Top performers in every field . . . are all more consistent than their peers. They show up and deliver day after day while everyone else gets bogged down with the urgencies of daily life and fights a constant battle between procrastination and motivation. While most people get demotivated and off-track after a bad performance, a bad workout, or simply a bad day at work, top performers settle right back into their pattern the next day. The Seinfeld Strategy works because it helps to take the focus off each individual performance and puts the emphasis on the process.[17]

Once we get our new business development habit on the right track and start to see results, we activate what Clear and others have described as the "habit loop"—a virtuous cycle of cues, cravings, responses, and rewards. A cue can be as simple as, "As soon as I pour my first cup of coffee, it's time to do my BD." A craving might be the desire to grow your pipeline of new opportunities. A response might be reaching out to several clients about new opportunities, and rewards might be landing a new piece of work because of your business development efforts.[18]

Habit 2: Prioritization

If business development rhythm is all about where *to* spend time, there is an equally important flip side: prioritization—or, where *not to* spend time. It turns out that Activators are as committed to the rhythm as they are ruthless about where they should not devote time and energy. One of the hallmarks of high-performing sellers is that they are better at prioritizing sales efforts than their peers. But prioritization is even more critical for doer-sellers in professional services. With so many competing demands on a professional's time—from client work to business development to firm-level projects and initiatives—it is of paramount importance that they avoid wasting their time on low-probability opportunities and activities.

Our research team at DCMi looked at specific activities performed by Activators as compared with those of average business developers. This was a complement to the time-spend analysis. Let's look at the specific activities and differences we observed:

Early-stage Activator activities:

- Targeted outreach strategies (including LinkedIn)

- Networking, especially at firm-hosted events

- Speaking engagements

Early-stage non-Activator activities:

- Blogs, posts, and bios

- LinkedIn thought leadership

- Raising internal awareness

The first thing to notice is that Activators are much more likely to engage in early-stage activity that has a known and named audience and represents a clear opportunity to build their professional networks. By contrast, average performers tend to send thought leadership missives out into the universe, hoping for a response.

There's a secondary challenge to the passive thought leadership approach: *you lose control over the next step.* To be clear, we don't mean that you should shy away from talking about your expertise. Instead, make sure that when doing so, you maintain control of the process. Because Activators do so only when engaging known and named audiences, they are in a much better position to follow up.

We see similar patterns in late-stage client development:

Late-stage Activator activities:

- Creating (and assessing) opportunities

- Targeted client and prospect contact

- Proposing work

Late-stage non-Activator activities:

- "Service account management" or internal servicing of rainmaker accounts

- RFP responses

- "Wishful" client contact (e.g., checking in with existing clients to see if there is additional work available)

Again, we see the difference between reactive and proactive approaches. Activators continue to suggest opportunities and propose new work while average client developers are stuck in RFP responses or stuck in "the friend zone": for example, client meetings with friendly contacts who are always happy to meet but never seem to lead to paid work. Once meaningful engagement has been established, we see even more targeting and prioritization from Activators. They are contacting based on a disciplined set of criteria and with a clear hierarchy in their contact list (much more to come on this in the next chapter).

Overall, when we look at Activator behaviors, what we see is a consistent pattern of more proactive activity, whether it is in early- or late-stage client development. They are more likely to instigate activity, whereas the average business developer reacts to a contact. By being more proactive, Activators have more control over the next step in the process.

Another aspect of targeting that is a strong Activator differentiator: the nature and shape of client portfolios relative to those of non-Activators. Every professional has a portfolio of existing clients that can be mapped according to average billings. A few clients will make a deeper investment or greater connection, and some will start with or naturally have lower billings because of the nature of the work being done. When DCMi looked at the distribution of an Activator's client billings versus those of the average professional, the difference was stark in two respects.

First, the average performers were much more likely to be burdened with a long list of clients with very low billings. For law firms, these might be clients for whom a professional has only $1,000 of work in a year compared with those with $10,000 or greater. Average performers were quick to defend these accounts, arguing that they had the potential to grow into more substantial relationships. But they also acknowledged that there was a lot of work involved in servicing these small clients.

By contrast, Activators are disciplined in reading the signals about client growth potential and, when necessary, transitioning them away or even suggesting an alternative firm. This does not mean Activators simply cut off *all* clients if they're not spending enough. Activators preserve important relationships and recognize that while a contact may not be a profitable client, they may play another important role in their network.

The other difference is that the client map for average performers looks like exponential decay—a very small number of clients providing the bulk of the billings, followed by the long tail of smaller clients. When we graphically depict the chart of an Activator's accounts, it resembles more of a cosine wave—a flat area of medium- to high-billing clients that extends further out before dropping off quickly. This means that, in practice, Activators have more midlevel clients with the potential to become big clients. In other words, they have a better pipeline of potential client work that may one day come to fruition.

Summary

Building a business development system is about creating a set of small, precise, and actionable habits, and then sticking with them over time. The two habits we covered in this chapter that are central to the "commitment" part of becoming an Activator are developing a defined, consistent business development rhythm and practicing ruthless prioritization of one's business development time-spend and efforts.

In the next chapter, we will cover the second defining element of being an Activator: connecting broadly and deeply. Carving out and protecting time for business development is a challenge for busy professionals for whom selling is only a part-time job. By taking advantage of habit-formation best practices, however, fee-earners can create a business development cadence that sticks in the long run. Prioritization is all about making thoughtful choices on where to spend the scarce time a professional has for business development. Activators are ruthlessly efficient in their time spend and don't fall prey to wishful thinking about long-tail clients that lack the potential to become sources of meaningful paid work.

— 3 —

How Activators Connect Broadly and Deeply

Michael R. Hess, a member at law firm Bass, Berry & Sims PLC, told us that he is a big believer in the power of networking as a way to feed his business development pipeline:

> One way I win business is by helping clients expand their own networks—and that's often nonlegal in nature. I call it *gratuitous connectivity*. I do a lot of "speed dating" with people in my industry. I'll go to conferences three to four times a year where I'll schedule twenty meetings in two days; I'll randomly send an email out to people to ask if they'll be there. These are typically not people I expect to do work for in the near future, but it lays the groundwork for doing business together later on down the road. Almost all of my client relationships today tie back to efforts I made five or ten years ago.

Kelly Kay, the global managing partner of the software practice at executive search firm Heidrick & Struggles, believes in the value of connecting clients with other colleagues across the firm. For instance, if he's speaking with a CEO who's considering forming an international leadership team, he will make an introduction to his international colleagues. Professionals in many other firms don't do this because they don't trust one another or because their compensation plan doesn't incentivize such behavior. But Heidrick & Struggles encourages and rewards this kind of collaboration within the firm. Kelly says this philosophy has led to significant new business for Heidrick as well as for himself and his colleagues.[1]

Tom Day, a partner at PA Consulting, used purposeful networking to create opportunities with a potential client at a consumer packaged goods (CPG) firm. Tom's team realized that its CEO was active on LinkedIn and started responding to his posts. One day, the CEO liked a reply from one of PA's team members. In a follow-up post, the team invited the CEO to visit the consulting firm's R&D lab. The CPG company's head of innovation began following the thread; then she liked another post, and her team reached out to Tom's to set up a visit to the lab. Thanks in part to those connections, the CPG firm engaged PA Consulting for a seven-figure deal, as well as two other large projects. "It's about getting to the right people inside a monster of an organization," he says. Had he pinged the CEO directly without help from his team, the effort would have likely gone unnoticed.[2]

Each of these are examples of professionals demonstrating the second pillar of an Activator approach: connecting broadly and deeply. Let's dig into what this means and how to do it.

Connecting on Multiple Levels

Activators connect both internally and externally, on multiple levels. First and foremost, like any good professional, an Activator's professional network contains a robust number of clients and prospective clients. But, unlike most professionals for whom these connections are nice-to-have, they are very much need-to-have for an Activator. Why? Because Activators operate more proactively, generating their own business opportunities from their professional networks as opposed to reactively responding to inbound leads handed to them by their firms—something we'll discuss more in the next chapter. What's more, because of the dynamic nature of professional networks—wherein contacts regularly change jobs, companies, and industries—these client opportunities naturally replenish themselves. And as we just discussed, because of their commitment to business development, Activators engage their networks with much greater frequency than the typical professional, which means that they are quickly spotting these critical job changes and acting on them proactively rather than waiting for a client to pick up the phone and call.

The second type of connection we find in an Activator network are key stakeholders within the client organization. These are not decision-makers or buyers per se, but members of the client organization whose input is often sought by the senior-most executive when making service provider decisions.

In *The Challenger Customer*, the authors revealed that in today's client buying environment, the most important factor for a decision-maker in selecting a service provider isn't whether the service provider is easy to buy from, offers compelling value for money, or even whether it's able to flex to a buyer's needs—it's whether that service provider has the support of the decision-maker's team.[3] Gone are the days when economic buyers and C-level executives made vendor selection decisions by fiat. Today, those decisions are based on team consensus.

Activators understand that in today's client buying environment, senior executives are less likely to put their thumb on the scale for them, irrespective of long-standing business or personal relationships. So it's imperative that they have robust connections not just with senior decision-makers. It's just as important—if not more important—to have a "zippered" relationship up, down, and across the client organization. Having these deep relationships doesn't only help on the front end when the client is evaluating service providers, but on the back end as well since they help protect an Activator from the inevitable executive churn that can leave even established incumbents out in the cold when the boss loses their job.

One senior partner we interviewed serves as the head of the oil and gas industry vertical for a major global advisory firm. He makes it a point to establish broad-based connections within his client organizations:

> In many of these firms, the CFO is looking for his or her team to weigh in before hiring an advisory firm like ours. So just focusing your energies exclusively on the CFO makes little sense from a commercial standpoint. But engaging the team and other stakeholders across the business pays off in other ways as well. First, you never know when the senior leader may leave the organization, and having strong connections beneath them makes for a smart hedge. And second, many of these supporting team members will go on to become senior decision-makers in other organizations and will remember that you invested the time to build a relationship with them early in their careers.

The third type of connection we find in an Activator's network are colleagues from their own firm. This might seem obvious, but in our research, we've found that the average professional has a surprisingly small number of their own colleagues in their LinkedIn networks. Despite mountains of research—most notably, the excellent work of Professor Heidi K. Gardner of Harvard Law School—showing the clear growth advantages of professionals who collaborate with their colleagues to deliver greater value to clients, most professionals tend to do the exact opposite.[4]

For the average professional—especially Confidants—client relationships are a zero-sum game. While a professional *could* generate more revenue for their firm and for themselves by bringing their colleagues into their client engagements, they often feel as if they have more to lose than they do to gain. *What if my colleague delivers subpar work? What if they don't handle the client with the same level of care and attention that I do?* the thinking goes. *If anything bad happens, it'll come back to bite me and I'll be on the outs with the client. I can't afford for that to happen after all I've invested over the years to develop this relationship.* Unlike most professionals who protect and hoard client relationships, Activators purposefully bring their colleagues into their client relationships. In our study, 73 percent of Activators reported that they frequently do this, as compared with only 29 percent of non-Activators.

Why is this? Because Activators understand what most professionals don't: when the locus of loyalty shifts from "me" to "we"—that is to say, when clients engage not just an individual professional but multiple professionals and practice areas collaborating to solve more complex problems—these relationships become stickier and more resilient. Gardner demonstrates that clients are far more likely to remain loyal when working with multiple professionals across a firm.[5] Not only are they stickier, but these types of client relationships are much more profitable. "For a firm," she explains, "the benefits of multidisciplinary collaboration are unambiguous. Simply put, the more disciplines that are involved in a client engagement, the greater the annual average revenue the client generates."[6]

The reason for this, Gardner argues, is that today's clients are prone to seek out the lowest bidder on individual, commoditized services like basic tax or intellectual property work, but they have a harder time bidding out complex, multidisciplinary work—for instance, how a company manages the tax implications of selling its intellectual property to a competitor.[7] And it's not just an Activator's *firm* that benefits—the individual professional does as well. Gardner found that professionals who collaborate with colleagues on client opportunities end up selling more of their own individual services to clients as well, since collaboration provides an opportunity for colleagues to see one another in action and build the trust necessary to confidently recommend a colleague to a longtime client.[8]

The final type of connection in an Activator network is outside experts. Unlike internal colleagues who are in the same profession (e.g., other professionals in the Activator's own firm), these connections are often in completely different professional fields. For instance, an accountant's outside connections might include lawyers, consultants, investment bankers, commercial real estate brokers, or engineers. Why would an Activator bother cultivating network connections outside of their field of business? Two reasons. First, these outside experts are often significant sources of referral business. Activators therefore manage their referrers with the same care and attention that they give to clients. Second, they play a critical role in an Activator's network because Activators define expertise far more broadly than most professionals. While Activators each have their own personal areas of expertise, they rely as much on their unique ability to be "general contractors" for expertise. Activators know that they don't have all the answers to every question, but this doesn't stop them from offering to help clients. Even if they can't help personally, they know that somebody in their network can. Clients come to rely on Activators for their ability to connect them with others who might be able to help address their needs. One such consulting partner told us,

> One of the things I pride myself on is that my clients regularly ask for my help on things I have no personal expertise in. But they still come to me because they know I can always help connect them with a trusted person from my network who *can* actually help them. Even when I don't personally get the work, I still benefit from it because they'll credit me with having helped them out—which dramatically increases the likelihood they will come to me for those things they know are in my wheelhouse.

Connecting Like an Activator

Let's look at the two critical habits that together underpin an Activator's connection ability: network management and stakeholder management.

Habit 1: Network management

An Activator's professional network is arguably their most important strategic asset. So not surprisingly, they are far more dedicated than their peers to building and cultivating their networks. But it would be incorrect to assume that this means Activators are simply looking to max out their number of LinkedIn connections or collect stacks of business cards at events. Instead, they take a purposeful method and approach to network management—one that they didn't invent per se but has its roots in evolutionary biology.

Dunbar's number. Robin Dunbar is an Oxford University anthropologist and evolutionary scientist who, in a groundbreaking paper, correlated the size of the neocortex—which evolutionary biologists consider an "older" part of our brains—to the size of social groups maintained by primates.[9] It turns out the neocortex plays a crucial governing role in social relationships. Beyond a certain point, it struggles to handle more than a certain number of social connections, and the group splinters. Dunbar used these results to predict the optimal social group size for human beings. His finding—which has since been dubbed "Dunbar's number"—was 150.[10] (Dunbar notes that the real number typically ranges from 100 to 250, with the average around 150.[11]) As Dunbar later explained, this is "the number of people you would not feel embarrassed about joining uninvited for a drink if you happened to bump into them in a bar."[12]

Since Dunbar's initial research, there have been more than 1,400 scientific papers published that have explored his findings, overwhelmingly supporting the idea that human beings have roughly 150 meaningful relationships. Dunbar's most substantial research project on this topic involved mobile phone accounts. His team conducted a study of six million mobile telephone numbers by accessing anonymized call records from a telecom company in a large European country. After filtering out toll-free calls, his team still analyzed roughly six billion calls. Relationships were defined as a call out and a return call from the same number across a one-year period. After looking at twenty thousand complete phone records, the team found that the average number of relationships for each caller was 130.[13]

History is also rife with examples of Dunbar's number. The size of neolithic villages from the Middle East was 120 to 150 people, judging by the number of dwellings.[14] In 1086, most English villages were on average 160 people, as recorded in the Domesday Book. In military units, a company typically contains 130 to 150 soldiers. The size of the average church congregation is roughly 150. A survey of holiday card lists (conducted before the social media era) found that the average number of cards sent per person was 154.[15] Even online virtual worlds tend to cluster around this size.[16]

People, of course, are not born with 150 meaningful relationships but, instead, grow into this number. In his book *How Many Friends Does One Person Need?*, Dunbar describes how, at birth, they have one or two. Friendships tend to expand during a person's teens and twenties. By their thirties, people tend to have about 150 connections, and that number changes little until people reach their late sixties and early seventies, when their number of connections starts to shrink as a result of natural causes. "If you live long enough," Dunbar quipped, "it gets back to one or two."[17]

A tiered set of relationships. One of the most interesting elements of Dunbar's research was his finding that there are rings of proximity within the 150 number and beyond. As he explains,

> That inner core—which numbers about five relationships—gets about 40 percent of your total social effort; and the next ten people further out get another 20 percent. Those fifteen people who are closest to you get 60 percent of your total social effort. These are the ones that matter. That inner core of five are the ones that affect your health and well-being and longevity. They are what I call the "shoulders to cry on," the people who will drop everything and come to your aid when your world falls apart. The wider group of fifteen are really the core of your social world. They buffer you against the general stresses of life and living in social groups.[18]

Our team at DCMi was curious as to whether this framework had application within the world of professional services business development.

FIGURE 3-1

The five tiers of an Activator's network

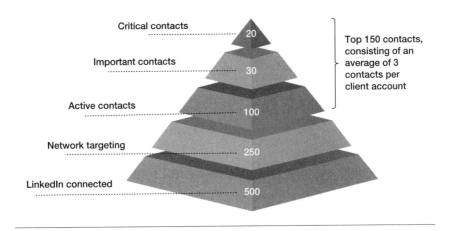

Using an AI-driven relationship intelligence tool from Intapp, we were able to map out the interaction patterns between Activators and their professional contacts. Specifically, we found that there are distinct tiers within an Activator's network, each of which has a different profile and set of characteristics as well as a different required engagement model—that is, a unique approach in terms of the "care and feeding" of contacts within it (see figure 3-1).

The frequency and nature of contact and engagement—as well as the subsequent reciprocity offered—increases as you move from the bottom tier to the top. Perhaps not surprisingly, we found that for Activators, their networks comprise not only external relationships but internal ones as well.

Our analysis showed that Activators have roughly 20 "critical contacts" who are their closest relationships; just below that, they have a tier of approximately 30 "important contacts." These 50 contacts are ones that Activators engage with high frequency and in a multichannel fashion. They text, call, or email critical contacts a few times per week and engage important contacts a few times per month. They meet in person with people from both tiers a few times per year, depending on their location. Below this tier are about 100 "active contacts" whom they engage quarterly. Beyond the top tiers are about 250 networking targets that Activators are engaging with on LinkedIn—liking, commenting, and sharing content to gauge the contact's interest in a live meeting (most often on a virtual platform but sometimes in person) and, finally, an additional 500-plus other LinkedIn connections.

Activators are extremely proficient at deciding who should be in their 150-person network. They are always evaluating when contacts need to be moved up or down based on criteria like fit and relationship strength. "Time is my scarcest resource. I have a ton of connections, but I can't spend unlimited time engaging with them and investing in the relationship if there is no real business opportunity," said one such Activator.

An important place for aspiring Activators to start in thinking about their 150 is by answering the question of who should be in their top tier. It's here where their time commitment—if misaligned—can cost them a lot. Too often, early career professionals take a "wishful thinking" approach to these connections, spending too much of their precious time on relationships that haven't shown promise but justifying it by thinking, "One day, they will become a great client." Activators know that they have finite time and capacity and are therefore ruthlessly disciplined about who they put in this top tier.

One question we often get from learners in our Activator training programs is: What are the types of signals that verify whether connections are, in fact, engaged and a good fit? Activators describe these connections as *authentic relationships*—those who are comfortable giving you feedback, who will reciprocate, who are happy to engage in an impromptu chat (often before or after business hours and even on weekends). Being on texting terms seems to be a litmus test that many Activators use. One told us "My closest contacts are the people I can text on a Saturday and they'll reply right back to me, and I would do the same for them." Some Activators reported that their innermost connections usually share some other social bond with them outside of work—a hobby, a favorite sport, or even having kids of a similar age. An Activator at a UK-based firm told us that all his closest professional contacts are people who are as passionate about cycling as he is. "It's clearly not the reason they work with me over other service providers," he explained, "but it creates a level of stickiness that paves the way for ongoing engagement and makes the work relationship fun for both parties. I think that's important."

The opposite also holds true, Activators told us: when connections you consider to be in your innermost circle don't reciprocate—when it feels like outreach is always coming from you and that you're somehow an imposition on your contact's time—then they do not belong in this relationship tier, no matter how much you would like them to. If it's unclear whether the relationship is of mutual importance, Activators suggest floating trial balloons like asking for a referral or a small favor to see if a contact reciprocates.

The importance of the bottom tier. None of this is to suggest that the bottom tier—our broader network of far-flung and diverse acquaintances—is not important to an Activator. In fact, quite the opposite. While Activators devote substantial energy to curating and managing their most meaningful 150 professional relationships, they also spend substantial time building and managing the bottom tier of their networks. And for good reason: research shows that it's the bottom tier—those with whom we have "weak ties"—that ends up being the most helpful for career advancement or generating creative ideas.

The seminal research on weak ties came from Stanford's Mark Granovetter in 1973.[19] Granovetter found that these relationships—more casual or loose acquaintances—were actually more helpful than closer ones in job seeking. This finding has since been replicated on modern platforms like LinkedIn. In one study, MIT and Harvard Business School researchers conducted a large-scale experiment over five years. Specifically, they adjusted the PYMK ("people you may know") algorithm so some people would receive weak tie recommendations and others strong tie recommendations. It was the moderately weak ties that led to the most job mobility; the effect was even more pronounced in digital and high-tech sectors of the economy.[20] Similarly, Markus Baer of Washington University found that networks with weak strength and high diversity offered more creativity, especially when the owner was highly open to new ideas.[21]

For an Activator, the bottom tier serves as their replenishment or feeder network. They regularly migrate connections in and out of different tiers—moving contacts from acquaintances to meaningful relationships and from meaningful relationships back to acquaintances. Sometimes these shifts result from a career or life change—for instance, if a contact moves into another industry, changes jobs, or retires. And sometimes they happen by design. Perhaps an Activator sees an opportunity to build a closer relationship with somebody who is currently only a connection in their bottom tier. Or maybe they aren't seeing the level of reciprocity that they would expect from one of their most important contacts and sense the need to downgrade the relationship.

The primary platform Activators rely on for managing their bottom tier is LinkedIn, and our data indicates that they spend significantly more time here than non-Activators. Seventy-four percent of Activators check LinkedIn at least daily (compared with 42 percent of non-Activators) and 32 percent engage their LinkedIn networks through posting, commenting, liking, or sending a direct message at least weekly (compared with only 10 percent of non-Activators who do this). In response to the statement "I make a concerted effort to expand the number of contacts in my LinkedIn network," 62 percent of Activators said they either "agree" or "strongly agree." In contrast, only 27 percent of non-Activators agreed.

To validate these findings and dig a bit deeper, we engaged in a separate study with the data insights team at LinkedIn, looking specifically at how Activators in professional services leveraged LinkedIn and its Sales Navigator tool in the last year, compared with their peers. We looked at the aggregate usage patterns of several hundred thousand Activators across various segments of professional services. The results were eye-opening. Overall, Activators perform six times more daily actions on LinkedIn than average (sixty per day versus ten per day for non-Activators). When compared with the average professional services user, Activators:

- Make 6.5 times more profile views per day (13 versus 2)

- Conduct 8 times more searches per day (8 versus 1)

- Save 31 times more leads/accounts on Navigator per day (8 versus 0.25)

- Send 10 times more direct connection requests per day (2 versus 0.2)

- Conduct 15 times more advanced people searches on Navigator per day (1.5 versus 0.01)

- Send 10 times more direct messages per day (2 versus 0.2)

- Make 5 times more new connections per day (2 versus 0.4)

- Share or post content 6 times more often per month (2.5 times versus less than 1)

- Get 8 times more inbound engagements off their content (40 versus 5)[22]

As a result of this time and effort, the bottom tier of an Activator's network ends up being significantly larger than that of a non-Activator. We found that Activators have 178 percent more LinkedIn connections than non-Activators. The average number of connections for Activators was just shy of 3,000, while non-Activators averaged just over 1,500 connections. More than half (57 percent) of non-Activators have fewer than 1,000 LinkedIn connections.

While LinkedIn is the primary social channel used by Activators, we see the same level of engagement and relative network size on other platforms. For instance, on Equilar's ExecAtlas platform—a popular digital platform used by professionals like executive search consultants and investment bankers who are looking to engage with top-of-the-house audiences like CEOs, CFOs, and board members who may not be active on

LinkedIn—we find that Activators track 20 percent larger networks of contacts and have nearly twice the level of activity of non-Activators.[23]

Live events like firm-sponsored or industry conferences also play a key role in an Activator's network management approach. Where most professionals spend their time standing off to the side, clumping with their colleagues, Activators work the event to establish new connections. We found that 80 percent of Activators attend events with specific goals as to how many new client connections they would like to make compared with 40 percent of non-Activators who approach events in this way. Seventy-eight percent of Activators go to an event with a specific target for how many post-event calls or meetings they will generate on the back end of the event compared with 34 percent of non-Activators who do this. And rather than simply collecting business cards, they work these new connections post-event: 78 percent of Activators track new connections they make at events in their firm's CRM system (versus 41 percent of non-Activators). Even when a new connection doesn't immediately convert into an opportunity, 99 percent of Activators report that they devote significant time to following up with and engaging these new contacts on an ongoing basis compared with only 73 percent of non-Activators who devote time to post-event engagement.

Once an Activator has targeted a contact to move into their 150, they try to move it from the place where the connection was first established—for instance, through LinkedIn or at an event—to a more personal channel such as a phone call, a virtual interaction like Zoom or Teams, or, ideally, a live meeting. As Dunbar and others have found, what maintains the tiers of your network and creates movement between them is the frequency with which you see and engage with these people. Social media can help, but it mainly helps us remember people. It won't in and of itself move a relationship across tiers. As Dunbar explains, "The layers come about primarily because the time we have for social interaction is not infinite. You have to decide how to invest that time, bearing in mind that the strength of relationships is directly correlated with how much time and effort we give them."[24]

Habit 2: Stakeholder management

The second key habit underpinning an Activator's approach to connection is stakeholder management. We know that building client relationships is a critical part of successful client delivery and therefore development. But which client relationships? Activators seek to create zippered connections within the client organization. They don't just target senior decision-makers such as C- or VP-level executives but also engage more junior members of the client's team who, while typically not the signatories on a purchase agreement, nonetheless play an important role in influencing critical decisions such as which service provider to go with for a given piece of work.

The problem of consensus buying. In an article published in 2012 in *Harvard Business Review*, a research team from CEB (now Gartner)—one that included coauthors of this book—revealed findings from several major quantitative studies of clients and how they buy. The researchers found that the average buying committee for a business purchase was 5.4 stakeholders—a number that has, since the original research was completed, increased to 11 and has been reported to be as high as 20 in some cases.[25]

Professionals we've interviewed as part of this research confirm that the number of stakeholders weighing in on service provider selection decisions has continued to escalate in recent years. Some of this depends on the nature and scope of the work being proposed. For a large-scale consulting engagement, there could well be a dozen or more key stakeholders, whereas for a smaller legal matter or executive search, there may be fewer. Geographic complexities can also factor into the equation: for instance, in Europe, it is often customary for all country heads to weigh in on significant purchasing decisions. But in general, most professionals agree that there are more stakeholders on the client side involved in service provider evaluation and selection than there once were. One executive search partner told us, "When I first started out as a consultant twenty years ago, I sold almost exclusively to the CEO or CHRO [chief human resource officer]. But today, I'm also having to sell to HR business partners, the HR operations leader, the head of recruiting, as well as lower-level HR staff and what feels like countless business partners who are influencing the decision."

This trend has accelerated since the pandemic, a period when all client interactions moved to virtual platforms and the cost of bringing together team members from disparate offices and markets effectively dropped to zero. "I feel like Covid was the thing that accelerated buying committee growth," said one partner we spoke to, "There's literally no downside to the client sending the meeting invite to everybody to get their perspectives on what we're proposing. It's not uncommon to hop on a call these days and find that the introduction portion of the agenda includes the client's team members introducing themselves to one another."

Consensus decision-making causes all kinds of problems for professionals trying to pitch their services into client accounts. The immediate problem is a greater burden on professionals to herd cats and manage complicated, multithreaded conversations when pitching for business. But as the CEB team's research also revealed, the problem is much deeper than just coordination.

With every incremental buying committee member, their research showed that the likelihood of getting a purchase decision from the client drops precipitously. Why does this happen? It turns out that while members of a buying committee can easily agree that there *is* a problem, they often struggle to agree on how best to solve it—let alone which service provider they should go with. The challenge of reaching consensus on how to move forward ends up being so onerous for many buying groups that pitches for new work often end up dying in committee—simply because of the internal dysfunction within the buying committee and their inability to agree on anything more than nonconfrontational options like saving money, staying the course, and avoiding disruption.[26]

Targeting the right client stakeholders. Activators know that to navigate the vagaries of today's buying committees, they need to find a champion on the client side—somebody who has the skill and will to get a dysfunctional group to agree on more than simply perpetuating the status quo. This is particularly important in situations in which they've proposed a significant piece of work (which is likely to attract more stakeholders to weigh in on the purchase decision) and in situations in which they're trying to dislodge a competitor (which is likely to draw out stakeholders who may be aligned with the incumbent provider). But who are these champions, and how does one find them?

Fortunately, the research by the CEB team yielded some answers to this question.[27] Their study of more than seven hundred client stakeholders found that client stakeholders fall into three broad categories—each of whom play a different role in a buying committee: "Blockers," who are defenders of the status quo (and often the individuals who advocated for the incumbent provider); "Talkers," who are friendly and can be useful sources of information but who are unlikely to stick their necks out for unpopular decisions; and "Mobilizers," who are skeptical and especially analytical but can be champions for transformative change—as long as they can be convinced.[28] The research showed that average performers tend to gravitate toward Talkers because they are friendly, accessible, and generally easier to engage than other stakeholder types, whereas high performers target Mobilizers who, while difficult to win over, have the wherewithal to generate consensus across a dysfunctional buying group.[29] This framework, developed by the researchers, is obviously most useful for professionals engaging multiple stakeholders and dealing with larger buying committees, but it's also a powerful lens to use when thinking about whether an individual client is inclined to champion us internally or just talk us to death.

Two words of caution in applying this research. First, be wary of assuming that senior leaders (e.g., the general counsel or CFO) will always be your champion. The researchers found that senior leaders were equally likely to be Mobilizers, Talkers, or even Blockers. Title, seniority, and role need to be ignored when you're hunting for a champion.[30] And, second, while a champion is clearly most valuable to a professional when work is being proposed and they need an internal stakeholder's help to get the buying group to move forward, this isn't to suggest that professionals should wait until they are pitching new work to find their champion. Here's why: one of the surprising insights that came out of their study was that buyers are 57 percent of the way through the purchase process before they ever reach out to a service provider to ask them for a meeting.[31] In other words, by the time they reach out to a professional or firm to ask for time or to invite the firm to participate in an RFP process, they've already done extensive research about how to solve their problem and which service providers should be on the short list. This means that most opportunities to earn new client work actually stall out or are killed *before* the client reaches out to a professional to ask for a meeting.

Activators avoid these traps by building deep relationships with the right kind of champions—wherever they find them—inside the client organization and doing so long before the client starts considering new projects and potential service providers. They do this by conducting relationship visits—not to pitch their services but to be front of mind before the next opportunity arises. This dramatically increases their odds of winning the next piece of work or their understanding of how to win it.

Summary

What does it mean to connect in the way Activators do? Activators know who the right clients are for them. They build a system of tiered relationships geared toward that fit. Their network ecosystem includes prospective clients as well as key client stakeholders, other firm members, and experts outside of their own domain area. They regularly engage their closest contacts and look for reciprocity in their business relationships, moving contacts up or down based on contacts' response to their engagement efforts. At the same time, they leverage social media platforms like LinkedIn to build a large bottom tier of connections that provide a feeder mechanism should one of their close contacts disengage for whatever reason.

Activators also engage in purposeful stakeholder management within client organizations, seeking to create zippered connections from senior leaders down to more junior team members and cross-functional partners. They do this because they recognize that purchase decisions are made by committee, and, as a result, they can ill afford to be exclusively focused on senior decision-makers who will, more often than not, turn that task over to their teams.

For an Activator, not all internal stakeholders are equally valuable in getting dysfunctional buying groups to coalesce around big decisions such as moving forward with an expensive proposal or switching from a long-established incumbent provider. Like any high-performing seller, they seek out the most effective champions within the client organization since they know that these individuals have the skill and—provided they can be convinced of the merits of a specific course of action—the will to get more risk-averse colleagues to move forward.

4

How Activators Create Value

Chuck Duross, a partner at law firm Morrison Foerster, spearheaded the creation of a monthly email that goes to his clients:

> Rather than chasing the headlines, which a lot of firms do, we started doing a "top ten issues" email. Clients read this because it covers a lot of issues in the market that they don't have time to research, and it's one email, not a constant barrage. It's way more efficient for in-house people who are really pressed for time and resources. It's predictable in its timing. It's useful and concise and links to all the source documentation, so if you want to go deeper on any of the topics we're covering, you can. It's been very successful. When our clients move jobs, it's pretty routine for them to ask to update their contact information so they can keep getting the monthly newsletter. It's a bespoke list of eight hundred to nine hundred people and our clickthrough rate is really high.

Susan is a partner in the tax advisory practice of a large global accounting firm. She sees it as her job to bring new ideas to clients—even when those ideas are outside her area of expertise:

For my clients who are members of in-house tax departments, it's about keeping them informed, keeping them abreast of the latest issues, sharing potentially valuable information. It's all about making them aware of something relevant to their job. If you do it well, it should lead to an expansion of the relationship. They trust you more as a result. And it's not just about me, it's about everyone in the firm. I talk to them about a wide range of topics, even things I could never advise them on. But those are topics that I can feed to other people. So it's much broader than just me. The corporate tax job can be quite lonely. You miss having someone senior to talk to about important issues. We have an office full of professionals they can talk to.

Muneer Khan, a partner at UK law firm Simmons & Simmons, talks about the importance of "paying it forward" to generate business:

I'm often asked for guidance. The first conversations are usually not charged for. The initial conversation is just getting to know you. Part of what I'm giving is my experience and guidance: Should they set up a presence in the UAE? Is it worth it? Can they do business in the wider region cross-border?, etc. I'm giving value immediately by providing the client with some initial views and pointers. Others in the market want the clock to start right away or they want something back immediately in exchange for offering advice. For me, I'm not expecting an immediate payback; it is about talking to people, learning about them, introducing ourselves, connecting them, pointing them in the right directions, and generally trying to help as many people as I can. When they can reciprocate, they will, and they often do.

These professionals are demonstrating the third and final pillar of the Activator approach: creating value for clients. As with the other chapters, we'll provide the research backing behind this concept as well as the key habits that support it.

A Unique Approach to Value Delivery

The idea of creating value for clients might strike readers as obvious—after all, any professional worth their salt creates value for their clients. But like the connect pillar we discussed in the last chapter, there's much more to this concept than one might think. Of course, Activators deliver value. What makes them unique, however, is *what type* of value they deliver to clients, *how* they deliver this value, and *when* it's delivered.

What to deliver

First, let's look at the *what* of Activator value delivery. In its simplest form, there are three ways that a professional can support and deliver value to a client. First is the impact of a professional's work on a client's business, namely, does their work help the client make money, save money, or mitigate risk? Second is the *way* in which a professional delivers work to a client and whether it is done in an honest, transparent, credible, reliable, and forthright way. In other words, does the professional do what they say they're going to do and is that work delivered in line with the client's expectations? And finally, a professional can support a client's personal goals and motivations. For instance, does the professional help the client manage their own career, gain new opportunities for visibility or advancement, or manage a personal or work challenge more effectively?

Most professionals are exclusively focused on the economic impact they deliver and the trusted way in which they deliver it (although it's worth noting that "technical professionals" like lawyers, accountants, and engineers can sometimes struggle to connect the dots between the work they deliver and the actual business outcomes that clients care about). And there's good reason to focus on these two dimensions. After all, if a professional cannot deliver business impact to their client or if they cannot be trusted by their client, they won't last long in the industry. But Activators see these two value dimensions as table stakes.

Activators recognize that there are many professionals and firms that deliver great work and do so with integrity. What sets Activators apart is the attention they pay to a client's personal goals and objectives. *Client-centricity* means something very different to an Activator. It means delivering value to the client's organization and helping clients to achieve business outcomes, but it also means delivering value to the *people* in the client organization: What are they trying to accomplish in their careers? What is exciting or challenging to them about their current role, team or organization? What's going on with them at a personal level that might represent an opportunity for me to help them? What are they passionate about outside of work?

This is not just the typical familiarity that many professionals pride themselves on, such as remembering the client's birthday and the names of their children. There's nothing wrong with this, but it's not the same as supporting a client's personal goals and objectives. This source of value is all about helping clients to achieve what matters to them personally. One Activator told us about how he helped reduce his client's workload by offering to provide feedback on his team members for use in annual performance reviews. Another—a partner in a consulting firm—leverages her firm's deep connections in the nonprofit sector to help her clients increase their personal impact on causes and issues they are passionate about—for instance, by finding opportunities for them to serve on nonprofit boards or sponsor fundraising events.

How to deliver

Next, there is the *how* of Activator value delivery. What's unique about the way in which Activators deliver value is that while value often comes *from* an Activator, it's just as common for value to flow *through* an Activator. In other words, Activators rely as much on their networks as sources of value for their clients as they do their own personal expertise. (See the sidebar "The Problem with Focusing Exclusively on One's Own Expertise.") This isn't meant to suggest that a professional's expertise is irrelevant or no longer important to clients. Far from it. The data shows us that Activators actually minor in the Expert approach.

But expertise, while necessary for success in professional service, is in no way sufficient.

Rather than claiming to have all the answers for the client, Activators see themselves as conduits for the answers—whether those answers are procured through a collaborative approach with colleagues or by connecting a client with outside subject matter experts from their professional networks. Practically speaking, this approach enables Activators to cover a much broader spectrum of client needs simply because they are harnessing the multitude of experts in their networks. This is reassuring and confidence-inspiring for clients. Just like a homeowner staring at the scary prospect of a major renovation, it's a relief to be able to rely on a great general contractor—somebody who can marshal the best architects, engineers, carpenters, electricians, plumbers, and masons to support the job.

One such Activator—an executive search partner—told us that she makes a point of providing extra support to executives she places in new industries:

> It's hard enough to switch companies as a senior executive but moving to a new company in a new industry is a "double jump" that many leaders struggle with. Let's face it: there isn't a lot of patience for highly compensated executives to learn the ropes on their new employer's dime, and these executives themselves often feel sheepish about asking basic questions of their new colleagues. So I always make an effort to connect them with industry experts in my own network who can confidentially coach and mentor them on the ins and outs of their new industry. This sort of thing has led to a lot of new work for our firm. These clients remember that we had their backs at a high-stakes moment in their careers.

When to deliver

The *when* of value delivery is also unique for an Activator. Where the strategy of the average professional is to wait for the client to find and reach out to them, Activators do the exact opposite. They proactively

The Problem with Focusing Exclusively on One's Own Expertise

Professionals who major in the Expert profile assume that the market will recognize their credentials and expertise and seek them out for it. But this assumption suffers from several fatal flaws—especially in today's client buying environment.

First, it assumes that the Expert's knowledge is so superior that clients will seek out only their advice. But we know that this is rarely, if ever, the case. As we've noted in previous chapters, by the time today's clients seek out the Expert for their advice, they are likely engaged simultaneously in discussions with other providers who claim to be experts in the same domain area. Sometimes these are professionals from direct competitors, but increasingly, they're boutique and niche service providers that the Expert has never competed against. In reality, expertise is never so exclusive as to preclude others from competing for the work.

Second, Experts assume that their expertise is so compelling that clients will seek out their advice proactively, before they have even determined what they need. Here again, Experts get it wrong. Because clients today often determine their needs in advance of engaging service providers, professionals are in the precarious position of having to react to a client's known needs as opposed to being able to shape the client's understanding of those needs. Not surprisingly, Experts end up being sucked into reactive pursuits—chasing RFP-driven opportunities that will largely be decided based on price. When clients are researching their own needs, they care

find ways to create value for clients and prospective clients in their network by curating information to surface issues and opportunities that clients might not yet be aware of but need to be aware of. They then target contacts for whom they think these insights are relevant and proactively engage them in a conversation to share their point of view. In our deeply about which professionals and firms might be the best fit. But once they create their short list of vetted service providers, they stop caring about who's best and focus mainly on who's cheapest and who will agree to their terms and conditions. In the client's mind, any of the providers who made the cut can do the work at the required standard. The real question is, who will be willing to do it for the lowest cost and most flexible terms? Experts therefore miss an opportunity to explain why they are best suited for the work by helping teach clients what matters most in a given engagement—and pull them away from price.

And finally, the Expert's approach is flawed because it assumes clients will compartmentalize their needs to fit the Expert's specific domain area and not ask for advice or support beyond their zone of competence. But the client's needs are rarely as straightforward as this. Instead, even seemingly simple engagements end up spanning multiple domains, requiring support that goes well beyond the Expert's specific area—to say nothing of larger transformation initiatives that definitionally cut across multiple functions. Yet because Experts (like most non-Activators) are generally reluctant to pull their colleagues into client opportunities, their value to the client ends up being greatly diminished, regardless of the depth of their personal capabilities. What's more, by sticking to their own knitting rather than trying to collaborate with their colleagues to deliver greater value to clients, Experts end up subjecting themselves to greater price-based purchasing. This occurs because an Expert's specific expertise is easier for a client to commoditize than more complex work that cuts across multiple domains.

research, nearly 60 percent of Activators reported that they frequently reach out to clients in their networks to make them aware of regulatory changes, court rulings, economic indicators, news events, or other trends and how they might affect the client's business. Only 34 percent of non-Activators reported doing this regularly.

Consider Eric Tresh, a partner at the law firm Eversheds Sutherland, who spends most mornings reviewing recent tax court decisions. He then identifies clients and prospects in his network for whom the rulings represent an opportunity or threat. He drafts messages to his connections in those organizations and proposes that they meet to discuss the implications. He understands that his clients don't have time to monitor the tax courts in all the jurisdictions in which they operate, so he does it for them. He doesn't do empty check-ins: he sends a message only if he truly thinks it's a relevant development. His clients tell him that when they hear from him, they know it isn't spam and that he's got something of value for them.[1]

There is a distinct pay-it-forward element to what Activators do. They approach these insight-based discussions with no expectation that they will immediately translate into paid work. Certainly, some of these outreaches will translate into real business opportunities, but even if they do not, Activators believe the effort allows a prospective client to get a feel for the value they can provide and can lay the groundwork for paid work down the road. This is akin to a product-led growth approach used by SaaS companies—only, in this case, the professional is the product. One firm CEO told us that his Activators "understand that billable work is what determines their compensation this year, and their unpaid efforts are what determine their compensation next year."

But there is also a practical element to what's happening here. In a market in which more and more client business is going through formalized purchasing processes, Activators are trying to get ahead of the RFP in order to shape the client's understanding of what issues they should be focused on, how to approach an opportunity, and how to think about a service provider's capability to support them. Ultimately, Activators are working to avoid situations in which the client's needs are *already* understood, and they are being asked to compete against other professionals and firms for the business. Our data illustrates this plainly:

- Seventy-three percent of Activators report that their preferred approach is to proactively reach out to a client to suggest an opportunity to work together compared with 36 percent of non-Activators who prefer to do this.

- Eighty-six percent of Activators frequently reach out to check on the status of an opportunity that they've previously discussed with a client as compared with 64 percent of non-Activators.

- Seventy-one percent of Activators frequently engage clients and prospects to see if they might need their firm's services compared with 27 percent of non-Activators who do this.

As we mentioned earlier, one of the questions we are sometimes asked is why we didn't simply call Activators Connectors—after all, one of their clearest defining attributes is their ability to build and leverage their professional networks. But this misses the central point of what it means to be an Activator. Yes, an Activator's network is central to their business development success, but it's merely a pipeline—albeit a powerful one—through which Activators flow value. This isn't to suggest that Activators don't share content broadly on platforms like LinkedIn—they do. But they aren't interested in collecting followers; they're interested in creating deep professional relationships.

Creating Value Like an Activator

Activators understand that it takes a critical pair of habits to proactively deliver value to clients: relationship development and insight development. Let's explore each in more detail.

Habit 1: Relationship development

There is widespread agreement in the professional services industry that the aspiration for any professional is to be seen as a trusted advisor to one's clients. But ask the average professional what that actually means and you're likely to hear a litany of different responses. Ask an Activator, however, and the answer is much more clean-cut: their definition centers around the need to flow or exchange value in the client relationship. To build a deep client relationship, you need to deliver business impact, you need to do it in a trusted way that supports your client's personal goals and objectives. We introduced this framework earlier in the chapter, but it is so central to the way Activators create value for clients—and so fundamental to their relationship development efforts—that we will explore it in more detail here.

What's most important to understand about this framework is that it is "MECE," or mutually exclusive, collectively exhaustive. Each element of this value equation, in other words, is independent of the others. As well, all three together explain the entirety of the value equation for a client—and, by implication, the entirety of what a professional must deliver to form a deep and lasting client relationship.

Many professionals who learn about this framework find it to be a relief. While mastering these three is difficult, the framework's simplicity is welcomed because it tells us that there are only three things that a client is looking for. It takes the guesswork out of relationship building and value creation. Over the years to come, you will find this framework invaluable. It will help guide the questions you ask your clients, it will help you demystify and make sense of their buying behaviors, and it will help you think about engaging your clients more generally for mutual benefit.

Let's double-click on each of these sources of value.

Economic impact. Economic impact is probably the most familiar to professionals. It can essentially be broken down into three drivers: increasing growth, lowering costs, and mitigating risk. These, in turn, are affected by the client's customers, the markets they compete in, their competitors, and their investors. In our experience, most professionals are readily able to point to examples where they help their clients achieve these business goals. But this isn't always the case.

One of the key skills that professionals must develop to identify the business drivers that are important to their clients is the ability to ask probing questions to uncover business needs. After all, sometimes the business reason behind a piece of work isn't as obvious or as simple as one might assume. Professionals can become so narrowly focused on the specific work they've been hired to do—for instance, conducting a search for a new executive leader, executing a deal, or implementing a new process or system—that they lose sight of how their work is tied to a client's business goals. And we often encounter professionals who think very narrowly about the business impact they're having. For instance, helping a client to identify and recruit a new executive leader might explicitly be about bringing in somebody to drive growth in part of the client's business or in a key market they compete in. But there is also an element of risk reduction to this work; namely, how will finding and securing the "right fit" candidate de-risk the client's growth strategy? Or, by contrast, what sort of risk would be incurred by bringing in the wrong candidate?

The problem for most professionals isn't that they don't know *how* to ask good questions, it's that they are uncomfortable doing so. Sometimes they fear that asking questions will "out" them as not being deep enough on the client's business and thereby limit their chances of success. One lawyer we worked with told us about the time he was invited to dinner and drinks by a friend in private equity and found himself to be the only lawyer in the room, surrounded by a group of private equity leaders. He was so concerned that he would be seen as an outsider that he didn't say a word throughout the entire event. What should have been a golden opportunity to make some new connections and start building new relationships turned into a bust. As he told us in a follow-up coaching session, "I feel like I should have interjected and asked some questions about how they think about their respective businesses. I wanted to jump in, but my fear of asking a naive question got the better of me."

Trust. The concept of trust in the relationship between professionals and their clients is not a new one. This idea has been explored extensively over the years—but perhaps no more so than in the work of David Maister, Charlie Green, and Robert Galford in their seminal book, *The*

Trusted Advisor. In it, the authors articulate what coauthor Green calls a "trustworthiness equation," defined as credibility plus reliability plus intimacy, divided by self-orientation.[2] Green explains that credibility is about knowledge, meaning that "the person is competent, capable, and has relevant credentials—perhaps they are a subject matter expert," while reliability deals with actions, meaning that "we can trust the person to do what they said they'd do." Finally, intimacy provides "emotional security in dealing with us. A high score on intimacy means we feel safe sharing information with that person." All three of these dimensions can increase a professional's trustworthiness. However, self-orientation, which comes down to "how much a person cares and shows awareness and interest in other people" can reduce trustworthiness.[3]

Another excellent framework comes from *The Four Factors of Trust* by the Deloitte duo of Ashley Reichheld and Amelia Dunlop. The authors argue that the ability of an individual such as a professional in a services firm to build trust is a function of their ability to be human (inclusive, empathetic, kind, vulnerable, and respectful), transparent (willing and able to talk about everything), capable (able to create solutions that deliver improvements), and reliable (taking ownership and delivering consistently and dependably).[4]

Over the years that we've been working with professionals, we've noticed that most have a pretty good sense of the importance of trust in building an enduring client relationship. But not many are fully aware of how critical it really is. While the Activator research shows us that trust alone is no longer sufficient to get the business in today's client buying environment, the absence of trust is a recipe for disaster for a professional.

If trust hasn't yet been earned, it's still possible to land a client's business. After all, it's hard to fully build trust without engaging in substantive work with a client. Most clients will say they have no reason to distrust a new service provider, but few will say they fully trust a professional until after they've engaged in a real project with them. Of course, once trust is lost or broken, the only way a client will continue to buy is if it is somehow captive (i.e., "We have no choice but to use you") but this is clearly not a safe place for a professional to be in. As soon as the client is able to switch service providers, they will.

Sometimes professionals misunderstand the nature of trust in a client relationship. It's less about avoiding dishonesty, selfishness, and manipulative behavior (though, obviously, those are surefire ways to break trust). It's more about putting the client first in even the most minor of situations—in other words, making clients feel like the only thing that matters to you is their success, not your own commercial objectives. Activators are acutely aware of the *agency dilemma* that exists between themselves and their clients: that is, the information asymmetry that can lead clients to feel that they're not being dealt with fairly or in an aboveboard fashion. As one consulting firm partner told us:

> Our clients hire us because we know more than they do about certain things and they need our expertise, but as important as it is to have expertise that your client wants to pay for, it's a double-edged sword because it can lead to the client worrying that you're not sharing everything with them. They know that we know how much things *really* cost, how long things *really* take, what project elements are *really* "need to have" and which are more "nice to have," etc. And so they worry that we won't be transparent about these things because they believe that it benefits us financially to not be completely transparent.

One Activator shared a technique he uses with new clients to overcome the agency dilemma:

> I make it a point very early on to share some things about our capabilities or our team, [which] sometimes surprises my clients because I'm being completely direct and honest with them. Clients are used to professionals being "bobblehead dolls," nodding their way through every meeting and claiming they can do anything the client asks. New professionals without an established book of business are especially guilty of this. But clients find it

genuine and refreshing to hear from a professional "You know, we actually aren't the best firm for that kind of work. We'd love to help you, but we'd recommend you go with one of our competitors," or "I know you want this to be done in a certain amount of time and at a certain cost, but I need to manage your expectations about how long this is going to take and how much it's actually going to cost."[5]

Trust can be built or broken at numerous points in a client relationship—and often in surprising ways. One law firm partner told us about a litigation effort he led on behalf of his client that resulted in a massive, eight-figure verdict in their favor. The client was thrilled with the outcome, and the partner assumed he and his firm were well positioned for providing support on future matters. But when the client completed the annual loyalty survey, he gave the partner and his team poor marks for their transparency and communications. The reason? The bill for the legal services provided ended up being 20 percent higher than what was originally estimated—even though the bill itself was a fraction of the amount the company won in the verdict. The partner told us:

> When I called the client to ask them for feedback, they told me that we should have been more transparent about the cost overruns instead of dropping a big bill in their laps at the end. I was a little shocked and explained that what they spent was a drop in the bucket compared with the amount we won for them. But the [general counsel] told me that budget management is on her team's annual objectives. The largest spend category for the department is outside counsel spend, and we had just blown their budget apart. They had missed a key objective because of it, which meant that some of their team wouldn't get paid their full bonuses. We eventually gave them a steep discount, but it wasn't enough to rebuild the lost trust. They haven't worked with us since.

One Activator we spoke with told us that she always sits down with clients at the outset of a project to understand what's important to them—whether that's budget, timing, resourcing, or outcomes.

> For the kinds of projects we do for clients, it's typical to have a weekly team call with the client to check in on progress, address issues, and so on. But for some clients, this is overkill; and for other clients, it's not enough. You could take the same project to one firm, and it's a minor initiative; while at another firm, it's seen as a "bet the company" undertaking. And that doesn't always map to the size of the client in the way you'd expect.

Another Activator we interviewed put it simply: "The key to building trust is recognizing that all clients have different expectations and never assuming you understand what those expectations are. The moment you start making assumptions about what's important to your client, you're in trouble."

Individual goals and objectives. Most professionals understand the importance of economic impact and trust to a client relationship. But few really understand the nature and importance of supporting a client's personal goals and objectives, which, according to Activators, is actually the stickiest of the three value drivers. This isn't to suggest it's the most important, but it is the most differentiating, the least likely to be commoditized, and when delivered properly, creates the strongest bond between a professional and their client.

The hard truth for professionals is that the ability to deliver business impact—while no trivial matter—is never exclusive to them or their firms. Many professionals speak about their differentiation, but no matter how specialized their skill set or how exemplary their credentials and experience are, they never exist in a category of one in the market. There is always another professional or firm that can claim, rightly or wrongly, that they can do the same work, and better or cheaper than you can. And although trust is central to building an enduring client relationship, maximizing trust is more about eliminating potential dissatisfiers and friction points in a client relationship. It's not a basis for differentiation. This is perhaps the best explanation for why Realists, despite their good intentions, don't perform as well as one might assume—because what they're trying to differentiate on is ultimately not that differentiating.

The second thing professionals get wrong is that they assume supporting clients on a personal level is about being *personable* with their clients; for instance, knowing that your client likes to play tennis and has three kids. Or they tend to assume it's about being likable or affable—being the sort of person your client enjoys spending time with. Those are good things, to be sure, but this value driver is all about understanding and supporting those things that are *important to your client as an individual.*

What do we mean by this? A simple framework is to think about the client and what they are trying to accomplish personally, either for themselves or their teams. For instance, on a personal level, clients might have any number of the following goals:

- I am looking to grow my network.

- I want to develop new skills.

- I want to advance in my career.

- I want to save time and be more productive.

- I want to be able to point to big wins for my team and company.

- I want to look like a hero for hiring you to do this work.

- I want to make my life easier.

- I am looking to advance the causes I care about.

And, from a team perspective, goals might include objectives like:

- Help me take pressure off my team.

- Help me to develop my team's capabilities.

- Help me to engage my high performers.

- Help my team to build department best practices.

- Help my team to better engage our internal business partners.

- Help boost my team's pride/confidence in the value they deliver.

- Help my team to work better together.

For clients, this is much deeper than being personable. When you get it right, it can create delighted clients who remain clients for the long run. Supporting a client's personal goals and objectives deepens a client relationship in ways that business impact and trust cannot. Delivering business results in a trustworthy way can make a professional a *trusted advisor*, but supporting a client on a personal level makes you their *ally*, which is something different entirely.

Without exception, the Activators we interviewed demonstrated a level of understanding and appreciation for the importance of this value driver in building deep, lasting relationships with clients. One strategy consultant told us that his client, the SVP of strategy for a large consumer packaged goods company, struggled to find time to coach new team members and worried that they wouldn't develop critical skills as quickly as she needed them to—and that the lack of one-on-one coaching she was providing would potentially drive disengagement and, ultimately, attrition. "The real problem for her," this Activator explained, "was that she needed her team to step up and be executive-facing. They were great analysts but struggled with synthesizing data and communicating recommendations effectively to the company's executive leaders. She didn't have time to teach them how to do this, given her own workload." The partner spotted a great opportunity to deliver personal support to his client and offered to run a series of presentation skills sessions for her team. "Each week, one of the team members presented a deck they were working on for an internal client, and the rest of us offered feedback and coaching. I was able to draw on my experience working with a variety of executive clients across industries. There was no prep required on my part, so it was a nominal time commitment. And, actually, it was a lot of fun."

A senior executive we interviewed shared a terrific example with us. Now the CFO of a publicly traded company, he told us about when he was the assistant controller at another organization several years before. His company had worked with a variety of executive search consultants to place high-ranking leaders on the team: the controller, the head of tax, and the chief risk officer, to name a few. He was always eager to talk to the consultants about his own career since he aspired to be a CFO one day, but none of the search consultants would give him the time of day. They were more focused on building a relationship with his boss—except for one. "This partner was one of the most respected in her industry, and she reached out to me to see if I wanted to grab coffee next time she was in town. I jumped at the opportunity. She could not have been more interested in learning about my own career objectives and gave me some terrific pointers that I firmly believe accelerated my own path to becoming a CFO." A few years later, he was promoted to controller at his company and the same search partner reached out to ask him if he wanted to be on a panel she was hosting at an upcoming industry conference. He was the only non-CFO on the panel. She spent time helping him prep, and he ended up making a big impression on the audience. One audience member recruited him to be their CFO. "The funny thing is that she didn't make a dime on any of this. She didn't even get the placement fee when I was hired as CFO, since the company used a different search firm. But I immediately brought her in and have now used her to hire all of the VP-level folks on my team since I've taken this role. I'll never forget what she did for me and my career."

One of the best ways for a professional to demonstrate support of a client's personal goals and objectives is their willingness to do off-the-clock work for a client. Clearly, there must be guardrails in place, but when clients feel like they can pick up the phone or fire off a text and get a quick opinion or word of advice from a professional, and not have to worry about getting a bill for it, it really cements the relationship value proposition. "The professionals I consider to be in my inner circle are the ones I can text anytime to get a quick opinion from, and they'll text me right back and not send me a bill for it," said one CEO we spoke to, "Those are the professionals who always get first dibs when I have paid work that needs to be done." One Activator we interviewed who owns his own talent consulting business told us that his job is to be an executive and career coach to leaders. But this isn't how he makes his money. "My day is full of conversations with leaders, none of which I get paid for," he joked. "But the vast majority of the leaders I've made time for have come back to my firm for paid work—and they all reference the fact that I provided value to them when they needed it most in their careers."

Sometimes the greatest form of personal support is providing reassurance and instilling confidence in your client. Jody Padar, a LinkedIn influencer known as "the Radical CPA" speaks about how CPAs can better manage and grow their firms. She shared a great example of this in a post:

> I sold my firm almost five years ago. This past week . . . two separate prior business clients reached out to me for business/tax explanations. Both of these prior customers have new CPAs and pay for their business books and taxes. . . . Yet for whatever reason, they didn't call their new professionals for help. . . . They don't *feel* connected to these new firms. They are paying for solid services, yet they are missing a connection where they *feel* their needs are being met. . . . All these two individuals wanted was a little conversation, explanation, and reassurance. When working with [small and medium-sized businesses] under $1 million in revenue, most of your job is explaining, reassuring, and listening. The taxes, the bookkeeping, and it being technically correct are table stakes.[6]

One final note about supporting a client's personal goals and objectives: it doesn't always have to relate to the client's work. Often, it can be delivered by better understanding and supporting the things that are important to clients outside of work; for instance, charitable causes, nonprofit board service, or philanthropic interests. One Activator we spoke to in our research, a UK-based management consultant, is passionate about men's health issues, having lost his father to prostate cancer. He's active outside of work in raising money for this cause and has found it to be a powerful way to engage clients who have been similarly affected by this disease or may have had a family member who has been affected.

Above all, the critical thing about this source of value is to remember that clients are human beings too. They've got their own goals and objectives, their own fears and concerns, and a life outside of work that is important to them. Activators recognize this and find active ways to support their clients in those areas that are often outside of the scope of paid work.

Relationship visits. DCMi's research with top client developers determined that it takes about four relationship visits to get one pitch meeting. Given this, relationship visits play a critical role in keeping things moving through a professional's sales funnel. These "pre-pitch" visits are a critical period for an Activator to identify their champion.

A relationship visit can take several different forms—it certainly is not just coming to an office to meet a client or picking up the phone. Such visits can and do include social gatherings, firm-sponsored events, and third-party events like industry conferences. The key is to understand the client's preferences (for instance, not every client enjoys attending sporting events or social get-togethers) and also to understand the objectives of the visit; namely, is it to build (or gain deeper knowledge around) business impact, build trust, or understand a client's personal goals.

For instance, in a social setting, it can be awkward (and even off-putting to the client) to try and gather information about business. But social gatherings and events can be great ways to build trust and understand a client's personal goals and objectives. Sitting next to a client at a dinner is a great way to discover areas to support a client on a personal level. In-person office meetings give professionals a chance to meet more stakeholders, get more of a sense for the company's culture, and learn what's going on in their business. This is when you're most likely to hear about specific opportunities to deliver business impact, often around issues you may not be the best fit for but for which you can source value from your firm or broader network. Hosting a client at a firm-sponsored event is a great way to build trust. If you're at one of your own events and looking good as a brand, you're building trust. And although Activators say that third-party events are most valuable for making new connections, they can also be a vehicle to attach other relationship visits. If one takes the time to look at who's attending and then sets up coffees, lunches, and dinners in advance, these sorts of conferences can serve multiple purposes.

In terms of guidelines for how often (and in what manner) to engage network connections, follow an Activator's lead. For the top tier (your twenty most important relationships as well as the next thirty):

- Engage in at least one to two contacts per month.

- Conduct at least one to two in-person relationship visits per year (as we discussed in chapter 3).

- Aim for multichannel engagement (phone, email, text, LinkedIn).

- Flag relevant news and events whenever possible.

- Look for ways to be personally helpful.

- Always tailor your outreach to the communication style and preferences of the client.

For the next one hundred relationships and beyond:

- Key targets should be getting regular (once or twice per quarter) outreach.

- Outreach should, as much as possible, be insight-led (e.g., "Other clients I'm working with in your industry have been focused on X" or "I thought of you because Y").

- Use outreach efforts to start a dialogue or set up a more substantive interaction (e.g., a virtual meeting or live visit).

- Take the time to comment on their recent LinkedIn posts or company events (i.e., don't just "like" posts).

One question we often get from our Activator training participants is whether live contact is required or whether a virtual meeting can be equally effective. Our view, backed up by the experience of Activators, is that while virtual has become a critical and acceptable medium in the post-pandemic work environment, if a professional is trying to send a message that a client is important and that they're looking to build a deeper relationship with that client, there's really no substitute for making the effort to visit in person.

Recently, we engaged with the key client team of a large accounting firm. We were coaching them on how to approach one of their top prospects—a major global bank. The client team had managed to secure a visit with senior leaders at the bank's New York headquarters. But because the firm's partners are spread out around the country, their inclination was to propose a Zoom meeting. "If we were you, we'd get on a plane and go visit them live," we suggested. "It's not really sending them the message that they are important to you if you default to the easy option the first time they offer to meet with you."

In this regard, overseas clients present a challenge for professionals but not an insurmountable one. Virtual will always be relied on more heavily when a client is located in a distant market. This makes it imperative that professionals find and leverage the few opportunities they will have to meet with their clients live—whether that's arranging a meeting when you're in the client's region or connecting at an event you both happen to be attending. One Washington, DC–based Activator has a heavy international client base. He told us that he books regular "business development trips" to key cities like London where many of his clients and prospects are based. "I carefully plan these trips and am quite literally booked from the moment I land until the moment I leave for home. I'll typically meet with at least five clients per day, but sometimes it's more than that. It's exhausting, but the face time we get is invaluable. I can say for certain that those regularly occurring in-person meetings have led to deeper client relationships for me and our firm."

Habit 2: Insight development

Clients despise "empty check-ins." As one client said in our interviews, "I find most requests to check in to be nothing more than a thinly veiled attempt to troll for more work. The professionals who do that don't actually care about me or my organization, they just care about my discretionary budget."

Activators don't do this. They set themselves apart by making sure their outreach and engagement efforts with clients are *insight-based*. Before we discuss how they do it, it's important that we differentiate between insight, thought leadership, and other forms of content.

In 2009, strategy guru Geoffrey Moore and his colleagues introduced a surprising and controversial approach to sales: rather than diagnosing client needs—as salespeople had been taught to do for many years—what if salespeople "provoked" customers with insights into *unseen or unknown* opportunities?[7] The authors called this approach "provocation-based selling." The objective of the approach is to "outline a problem that the customer is experiencing but has not yet put a name to."[8] Executed well, they hypothesized, a provocative insight could help to differentiate a supplier and spur a reluctant customer into taking action when they might otherwise not have been predisposed to.

Independently, researchers from CEB (now Gartner)—including several coauthors of this book—had launched a large-scale study of sales professionals, publishing the results in *The Challenger Sale* in 2011. The research revealed that client purchase preference was largely a function of the ability of a salesperson to deliver unique insights as part of the sales conversation.[9] The ability of a seller to show up with new ideas for how the client could make money, save money, or mitigate risk had more statistical impact on a client's purchase decision than the vendor's brand, reputation, product quality, service quality, or value-to-price ratio *combined.*[10]

The authors argued in that book and its sequel, *The Challenger Customer*, that insight differs from classic thought leadership in two key respects.[11] First, unlike thought leadership, which is designed to demonstrate credibility and therefore tends to be confirmatory, insight is revelatory.[12] In other words, it is surprising and designed to change the client's understanding of what the "right answer" is for their organization. Second, executed well, insight leads to the vendor's unique capabilities.[13] Unlike most sales content in which suppliers lead with their differentiators, insight seeks to disrupt the client's understanding of their needs in a way that creates demand for the vendor's capabilities. As the authors explain, [these insights] must tie directly back to some capability where you outperform your competitors. If what you're teaching inevitably leads back to what you do better than anybody else, then you're in a much better position when it comes to winning the business. We often put it like this: The sweet spot of customer loyalty is outperforming your competitors on those things you've taught your customers are important."[14]

These findings have since been confirmed in numerous follow-on studies. In their book *Insight Selling*, sales experts Mike Schultz and John Doerr found that across forty-two attributes demonstrated by sellers in their customer interactions, the attribute most frequently demonstrated by winning salespeople was their ability to educate the customer with new ideas or perspectives—which, it turns out, was the least frequently demonstrated attribute among second-place finishers.[15]

Insight in B2B sales interactions. We find that professionals and firm leaders often struggle with the concept of an insight-led commercial approach. To help ground this concept, let's consider an example from the B2B sales world—far outside the world of professional services.

A 2011 *Harvard Business Review* article shared the story of Grainger, a distributor of maintenance, repair, and operations (MRO) supplies. In the past, Grainger reps led with facts and figures about their company— how old they are, how many items they stock, how many distribution centers they have, and so on, all leading to the inevitable "So that's who we are. Now tell me, what's keeping you up at night?"

By 2011, a conversation with a Grainger rep was very different. It focused almost exclusively on a series of proprietary insights Grainger had developed about its customers that prompted them to think very differently about how to manage their MRO spending—in ways that could potentially save them millions. Rather than trying to convince customers to go with Grainger as their supplier of choice for planned MRO purchasing (which inevitably would lead to a price-focused discussion), Grainger reps started by showing them how much money they were likely wasting every year on unplanned purchases, which Grainger's research showed could be up to 40 percent of the average company's MRO spending.

No supplier wants to be in the business of free consulting—and Grainger was no different. The key is to teach in a way that leads customers to its unique benefits as opposed to leading with them. After reframing the way customers thought about MRO spending, Grainger reps created an opportunity to talk about a set of capabilities they could offer to better manage that spend, ultimately leading to higher-level sales conversations and bigger deals.[16]

Building and deploying insight in professional services. Delivering revelatory content in professional services is, in many aspects, about alerting clients to issues, risks, and opportunities before they've spotted them. Court decisions, regulatory changes, disruptive technology shifts, and M&A transactions are just some of the opportunities to alert customers to changes in the market that might have bearing on them.

Another form of insight is contextualizing firm-level thought leadership. This could mean the professional putting their own spin on their firm's content or directing clients to specific pieces of information or takeaways. One Activator said his most impactful outreaches start with the phrase "I thought of you because. . . ." This phrase, he explained, signals a level of thoughtfulness, foresight, and an understanding of the client's unique needs. "My clients are bombarded with generic thought leadership and other news alerts. It's a real value-add to synthesize this content for them and contextualize it for their role, company, or industry."

Activators counseled against two mistakes most professionals make with respect to firm thought leadership: spamming clients with as-is content or not sending it at all. Both represent errors in judgment and a lost opportunity to set themselves apart. Insight isn't something professionals need to have all the time. But it helps them stand out in a crowded market in which most players share equally impressive credentials and similar expertise.

From a stylistic standpoint, professionals should take care to push clients' thinking gently and respectfully and to avoid making it their "always on" posture, which—as the underperformance of the Debater profile clearly demonstrates—clients of professional services firms have no patience for. At the same time, when they do spot an opportunity to bring a new issue or idea to a client's attention, professionals should not hesitate, even if the client is likely to be challenged by the suggestion that they may have missed something or that they might not be thinking about an opportunity the right way. When given the choice between two professionals—one who merely looks to reactively address the client's known needs and one who brings new ideas to the client when the situation demands it—clients will invariably choose the latter. As one client said, "I rely on the professionals I hire to help me look around corners. I don't know what I don't know. They'll talk to more executives like me in companies like ours in a week than I'll talk to all year. So if I'm missing something, I need them to bring it up with me proactively."

An insight-development framework. While the way insight is developed and deployed in professional services differs in some respects, the core tenets remain the same. First, as *The Challenger Sale* authors argue, an insight-based message must guide a client to what the professional or firm does uniquely well in the market. Unfortunately, the vast majority of their messaging we see, especially in pitch decks, is entirely focused on the firm's capabilities and the professional's credentials. Identifying what you should be guiding your client to requires professionals and firms to understand what makes them unique. Deb Oler, former president of Grainger Brand, explained that the first step in identifying one's core differentiators is answering a seemingly simple but deceptively tricky question: "Why should our clients buy from us instead of our competitors?"[17]

To aid in this process, consider a simple framework. Imagine a Venn diagram with three overlapping circles: one is the client's known and unknown needs, the other represents what the firm's competitors' capabilities

FIGURE 4-1

Identifying your unique value proposition

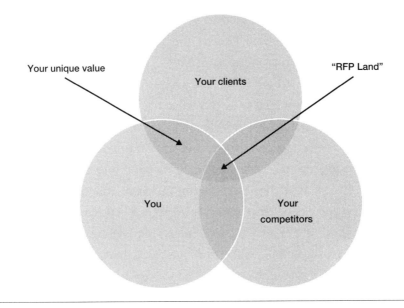

are, and the third circle represents the professional and their own firm's capabilities (see figure 4-1). What most firms do is lead to the center of the Venn diagram where they and their competitors are equally well-suited to address the client's needs—an area we like to call "RFP Land," where vendors will race to the bottom on price and the lowest-cost provider invariably wins. The best professionals and firms instead focus their client engagement efforts on the capabilities that overlap with the client's needs but are not shared with their competition. This is the area of competitive differentiation and represents the answer to the question posed by Oler.

One additional pointer: before concluding that you've identified your unique differentiators, it is wise to test your conclusions by asking three follow-up questions:

1. Is this capability ours alone?

2. Is this capability one we've delivered before?

3. Does this capability address a critical client need?

Professionals and firm leaders often erroneously conclude that generic capabilities—being innovative, entrepreneurial, or client-centric—represent unique benefits to emphasize in their messaging. But these claims inevitably fail the three test questions. First, for a capability to be able to be held up to clients as a unique benefit, it cannot be the sort of thing that competitors, rightly or wrongly, claim as well. If they do, it fails the test of uniqueness. Second, to be credible, it must be a capability that the professional or firm has leveraged to deliver value to clients in the past; and ideally, those clients should be willing to attest to that fact whether through a case study, a testimonial, or a reference call. And finally, it's all well and good to have unique and credible capabilities, but if they don't address significant risks, threats, or opportunities for the client, clients are unlikely to see them as valuable—and certainly are unlikely to pay a premium for it.[18]

Getting this right is hard, and we have seen professionals and firms struggle to clearly articulate their unique value, but being able to do so provides them a massive advantage. And those who market this value to clients should be able to pave the way with this strength as well (see the sidebar "Insight Development for Marketing Teams"). One word of advice before heading down this path: increasingly, differentiators are found in the *way* professional services are priced and delivered, rather than in credentials or experience alone. For instance, we have seen consulting firms differentiate based on how they combine their expertise in specific domain areas to create a "one plus one equals three" value proposition for clients looking to drive larger-scale transformation initiatives. We've also seen law firms differentiate on the fact that they have in-house alternative service providers who enable them to lower costs for clients on more commoditized components of legal matters. And each day, we are seeing firms announce new, proprietary, AI-based technology solutions that will afford additional opportunities to differentiate their value propositions in the market.

Implementing an insight-based approach to client engagement. An insight-based approach is, at its best, about bringing a fresh perspective on a problem the client may or may not know that they have, which forces

Insight Development for Marketing Teams

Insight is a powerful concept not just for professionals but for marketing teams in professional services firms who have long been focused on pumping out volumes of thought leadership that typically fail to change the client's mind or create a different impression with them and, unfortunately, serve to reinforce the client's perception that partners and firms are generally all the same. This can be especially dangerous when a professional is trying to dislodge an incumbent provider and trying to create white space between their firm and that of a competitor.

The questions marketers should ask about any content they put out for clients are: first, "How does this content connect to our unique capabilities (which, of course, presupposes that the firm knows what its unique benefits are)?" and, second, "What are we saying in this content that will disrupt or differently shape the client's point of view about this issue or opportunity?" Then, before disseminating to professionals, any content should be paired with a "just add water" playbook that makes it easy for them to post on LinkedIn, send an email, or pick up the phone to engage in a conversation with a client.

them to focus on alternatives to the status quo. But insight-based engagement presents other benefits to professionals as well, including:

- Helping professionals avoid the awkward "transition to business" moment in a client interaction (i.e., getting out of the "friend zone")

- Setting up value-based information exchanges between professionals and clients

- Creating a natural occasion for cross-selling and collaboration rooted in a client-centered value discussion

One word of caution for professionals looking to engage clients in an insight-based way: don't let the perfect be the enemy of the good. Professionals often struggle, sometimes for weeks or even months, to come up with the perfect insight. In the meantime, they remain silent and don't engage the client at all. This is clearly not the outcome that professionals—or clients, for that matter—want.

The biggest complaint we see in our voice-of-client data is that clients wish they heard from the professionals they work with more often. They value their unique perspectives on the market. They aren't simply OK with hearing from professionals between paid engagements—they expect to. Clients are desperate for insights, and they know that the professionals they work with have a broader perspective and often more expertise than they themselves have. Clients consistently lament that they can't see around corners. They are looking for professionals to be thought partners, sounding boards, and confidence-givers as they struggle to navigate the complexity of the current business environment.

So, given a choice between sending an imperfect outreach or sending nothing, professionals should err on the side of early and frequent engagement. One Activator we interviewed in the executive search space told us that she is perfectly comfortable sending short emails, texts, or LinkedIn messages to clients to get a conversation—even if she hasn't yet fully baked her insight on the subject or how it connects to her or her firm's capabilities: "If I see something in the market—a big hire, a major transaction, or a piece of talent-market-related news—I use this as an opportunity to engage with current clients and prospects, even before I've figured out what my own personal angle is on the specific issue. It's always better to engage now than putting it off for later."

Summary

Activators demonstrate two clear value-creation habits: First, they are as focused on understanding the personal goals and objectives of their clients as they are on the business and trust elements of the relationship, which clients expect of any service provider. Second, Activators look to bring insight, not just information, to their clients. Ideally, the insights they bring help to reframe the client's understanding of a threat or opportunity in a way that leads to the professional's and firm's unique capabilities. But, at the very least, Activators always strive to make value the centerpiece of any client interaction. As one Activator aptly said: "I never reach out to a client unless I have something valuable to offer or something important to discuss with them."

— 5 —

The Activator Mindset

As you consider how you'd like to apply the lessons from this book, a perfect place to start is here: understanding how the right mindsets can enable and support the adoption of Activator behaviors and habits. Start thinking like an Activator, and the rest will more easily fall into place.

Activators share three mindsets that underpin their business development habits and their client engagement approach: self-determination, other-focus, and resiliency. These are switches that all Activators have successfully flipped to the "on" position. Without them, Activator habits won't stick and, ultimately, they'll fail to distinguish themselves in the moments that matter in the client relationship.

Lest readers become discouraged, it's important to distinguish between a mindset and a personality. The American Psychological Association (APA) defines *personality* as "the enduring configuration of characteristics and behavior that comprises an individual's unique adjustment to life, including major traits, interests, drives, values, self-concept, abilities, and emotional patterns."[1] In layperson's terms, our personality is the combination of characteristics that make us who we are as individuals. As such, it's deeply ingrained and, to the extent that it can be changed—which remains a hotly debated topic among psychologists—any change is gradual and difficult.

Mindset is very different. The APA defines it as "a state of mind that influences how people think about and then enact their goal-directed activities in ways that may systematically promote or interfere with optimal functioning."[2] Unlike personality, there is general agreement among psychologists that people can adopt new and different mindsets to help them navigate through challenges or adapt to different life or work circumstances. Mindsets are more flexible and can be changed through training, coaching, and other development experiences.

A question we often hear is whether introverts can become Activators—after all, Activators are the professionals who are comfortable networking and working the room at events. Of course, the answer is "yes," because what makes one an Activator is distinct from one's personality. Introverts and extroverts are equally capable of building networks and delivering value through those networks as general contractors for expertise. Given that large social events are more likely to drain energy for introverts, however, they most likely use network-building approaches that are more one-to-one. Or they are even more careful to prioritize their social interactions to those who are most important in the network. But they are still Activators because they follow the mindsets, habits, and behaviors that are part of this proven client engagement approach.

One Activator we interviewed, who is an admitted introvert, would attend client events regularly but would invariably skip the evening cocktail hour. "You won't find me at the bar at client events. I'm always back in my room by 9 p.m. every night" she told us, as she knew that would give her the energy for the scheduled meetings, lunches, and new connections across the next day. More important than the evening social hour was her regular value-led follow-up after the session and ensuring that those new contacts became LinkedIn connections and, ultimately, business opportunities.

We've seen in our own training programs that any professional can learn to change, adapt, and improve their business development approach. But it all starts with having the right mindset, so let's dig into each of these Activator mindsets in more detail.

Self-Determination

Most professionals believe that business development effectiveness is largely out of their control. Some, particularly firm leaders, subscribe to the view that business development skills are innate; that is, a professional is born with them or not. Others believe that business development success is a matter of luck—that the best were fortunate enough to get assigned to a big account or inherit a large client from a retiring mentor. And still others believe that business development is ultimately in the hands of the client—that is to say, that clients buy when they have a need and that there's little a professional can do to create a need where none naturally exists. Perhaps most disheartening, many professionals we interviewed shared that they see business development as a dog-eat-dog pursuit where some fortunate colleagues are able to grow a successful practice while others are not—and that those who are successful often accomplish this at the expense of their colleagues.

Activators do not subscribe to any of these beliefs. Instead, they practice a mindset of *self-determination*: the belief that their fate is in their own hands—that they are in control of their own destiny as business developers.

Self-determination theory holds that human beings have three basic psychological needs:

- The need to be autonomous (i.e., the feeling that one has choice and control over what one does)

- The need to achieve competence (i.e., the feeling that one can achieve mastery over what one does)

- The need to experience relatedness: (i.e., the feeling that one is connected to others in a shared purpose)[3]

Each of these dimensions can be seen in the way Activators approach business development—and, in fact, the opposite can be observed in how non-Activators approach the commercial aspects of their roles.

Activators reject the notion that business development results are a matter of luck or circumstance. They do well not because they were in the right place at the right time but because they put in the effort to generate the results they're after. Unlike the many professionals (especially Confidants) who told us that they inherited their biggest client accounts, every Activator we spoke to told us that they built their book of business through having a clear strategy, their own hard work, persistence, and dedication to developing client relationships. Luck, as they see it, had little, if anything, to do with it.

Activators also don't believe that business development happens on the client's terms. Because most non-Activators are lacking in self-determination, they believe their business development success is in the client's control. They believe they can only generate business when the client needs their help. Activators believe that they can bring ideas to clients and create demand where none was thought to exist. In this way, they believe they have autonomy over whether they are commercially successful or not.

Second, Activators do not believe client engagement and business development are innate skills. They see them as capabilities that can be mastered by anybody with the right commitment to training and practice. Across the board, Activators told us that their results are a function of hard work and commitment to becoming good at business development. Several admitted that business development wasn't something that came naturally to them and that they struggled before they figured it out and ultimately found success.

And finally, Activators believe that business development is a shared pursuit, not a zero-sum game in which some professionals win and others lose. Whether they are compensated explicitly to do so or not, Activators see business development as a team sport. One Activator told us he'd recently landed a huge, nine-figure client opportunity that would leverage a whole host of his firm's capabilities and took months to bring across the line—but wouldn't benefit him personally, given the way the organization's compensation system worked. "Regardless," he said, "I would do it all over again."

Simply put, the Activator's mindset is that when they commit to business development, the results will follow, and the positive outcomes will be felt broadly across their firm. This is quite different from the typical professional who believes that success or failure is beyond their control, that external circumstances such as market forces or changing client preferences will determine their fate, and that success, such as it is, is theirs alone.

One final point regarding self-determination that shouldn't be overlooked: people who feel they are in control of their own fate—who have a sense of autonomy, mastery, and relatedness—tend to be much happier than those who feel that their fate is controlled by others. And while this isn't something that we tested for; it was something that came through clearly in our Activator conversations. Take, for instance, the legal profession. The ALM Mental Health and Substance Abuse Survey found that 31 percent of lawyers report some sort of depressive disorder compared with an average of 7 percent for the US population.[4] But our discussions with Activator lawyers, as well as those in the other segments we studied, felt different. These professionals came across as buoyant, confident about their chances of success, and excited about engaging in the hard work of client development—not at all the picture of the discouraged, helpless professional at the mercy of the client or the market. When we shared our insights about the declining state of client loyalty with an Activator from a global management consulting firm, for instance, she took a decidedly glass-half-full, if not optimistic view:

Clients will never stop changing how they engage us or raising their expectations of us—nor should they. It's healthy for me, for my colleagues, and for our firm to be pushed to compete more effectively in the market and to deliver more value to our clients—whether that's demanding new, innovative solutions from us or looking for us to collaborate to solve more complex problems. When we do this, we win and our clients win as well.

Other-Focus

When we ask learners in our Activator training programs what they think it means to be *other-focused*, the most common response we hear is "client-centric." Perhaps it seems obvious. Any successful fee-earner in professional services—in any form of persuasive endeavor—has to put themselves in their clients' shoes. But there are nuances to what client-centricity means for Activators.

Being a subject matter expert—which all professionals (and not just those in the Expert profile) are—requires confidence and can encourage tuning out individual client context; fear of exposing a lack of understanding and perhaps losing credibility tends to make professionals avoid delving deeply into client issues. As a result, the average professional is usually focused more on trying to prove their expertise than they are on helping clients accomplish their own objectives. And they tend to focus narrowly on how to do the specific things they've been hired to do rather than more broadly understanding the context surrounding the assignment. It takes a deliberate mindset shift to move into curiosity and empathy and explore the full context of the client's issues and personal objectives.

For an Activator, client-centricity is more than good service or being attentive: it's about demonstrating genuine empathy—but not the sort of *emotional* empathy many of us are familiar with. Instead, we're talking about *cognitive* empathy. Recall the three reasons clients buy: a professional's ability to deliver economic impact to the client's business, their ability to deliver work in a trusted manner, and their ability to support the personal goals and objectives of a client. Activators think about all three elements to really uncover the reasons the client needs their help and hired them specifically for the work. They ask themselves: *What is the full business context surrounding the specific piece of work? How does this assignment factor into the client's broader business strategy? How does it tie into the client's other ongoing initiatives or projects?* They also try to understand the delivery parameters that are important to the client so that they don't breach the client's trust: *What is the client's budget, and how sensitive are they to potential overruns? Are there time constraints I need to be aware of? What is the frequency and level of detail they're expecting in terms of project updates?* And, finally, they try to understand the client's personal goals and objectives that might be in play: *What is the client trying to accomplish personally or professionally? Can I help them to achieve those goals, whether through this project or some other means?*

This sort of cognitive empathy is essential to business development. Our team heard countless stories from Activators describing how they handle difficult conversations with prospective or existing clients. One professional told us about an engagement that was running behind schedule and over budget due largely to unforeseen system integration issues on the client side:

> From our perspective, this sort of thing happens fairly often. We were pretty unfazed by it. But our client was distraught. Some members of our team thought the client was being unreasonable and were inclined to just tell him that delays happen. But I suspected there was more to it. When we sat down to discuss the project issues face-to-face, I learned that he was up for a big promotion and his boss had given him responsibility for this project as a way to prove himself and that the cost and time overruns would reflect badly on him. It gave us a very different appreciation for what the client was going through and led to some creative problem-solving on our side—for instance, leveraging our offshore team so that we could work around the clock and keep the costs in line—that I don't think we would have gotten to had we not taken the time to understand the entire context of the situation.

In each of these cases, the Activator would describe how the client's whole demeanor would change when they took an empathetic posture that demonstrated a real understanding of the client's value drivers. It no longer felt like the conversation was a battle but rather returned to a conversation or joint problem-solving effort.

How do Activators adopt an empathetic posture with clients? In her book *The Empathy Effect*, Dr. Helen Riess, a medical doctor from Harvard, identifies several scientifically derived elements of empathy, including posture and affect.[5] We hear Activators talk about both of these in our interviews.

In terms of posture—that is, how one's views are positioned relative to the client—Activators would talk about how important it is to be on the same side of the table during difficult conversations. In one interview, an Activator described how, on a call with a client who was upset about having to explain unbudgeted costs to his boss, instead of battling the client on the facts of the situation, she stopped, thought about the uncomfortable position her client was in, and simply said, "I understand that we put you in a tough position. How can we give you some wins to help you navigate through it?"

Identifying and naming the emotions you perceive in others—that is, their *affective state*—is also a technique that Activators use to stop themselves from rushing into the conversation with their own perspective or becoming defensive. Perhaps most important from a business development perspective, especially in a difficult conversation about fees, is to "hear the whole person." This means stopping to ask, "How is this [problem/issue/question] going to impact you personally or professionally?" Stepping back to understand the full picture not only demonstrates empathy and makes your counterpart more likely to listen in return—especially in difficult situations—but also can give critical insight into solutions.

Fortunately, there is good news for anyone who doesn't have this mindset: research shows that it can be learned. For example, multiple studies have shown that interventions to improve physician empathy are largely effective.[6] One of Dr. Riess's studies used empathy training to, among other things, improve physician awareness of patients' emotional verbal and nonverbal communications to better manage challenging interactions.[7] The result was a change in patient ratings of physician empathy that was statistically significantly greater in the training group as compared with the control group that received no empathy training.[8]

Being other-focused doesn't only describe an Activator's mindset regarding clients and client interactions; it also describes their mindset with respect to their colleagues. Most professionals—especially Confidants—tend to hoard client relationships. They do this not because they don't believe their clients would value a more collaborative, "one firm" approach to addressing their needs, but because they fear the negative fallout that could ensue if a colleague delivered bad work or otherwise ran afoul of the client.

Activators, by contrast, demonstrate a distinct *pride* in others that is seen in their far greater willingness to bring their colleagues into client opportunities. To quote one Activator we interviewed, "I never shy away from making introductions for my colleagues if for no other reason than the fact that *I know* they're going to have a great conversation with one of our partners and they'll thank me for making the connection."

Resiliency

The third defining mindset of the Activator is resiliency. *Resiliency* is the degree to which a person bounces back quickly from criticism, rejection, or setbacks. Often paired with buoyancy—what Dan Pink called one's ability to float "in an ocean of rejection"—resiliency is the other side of the coin: the ability to keep pushing through to pursue the business even after an initial rejection or no answer.[9] As one high-performing Activator told us, "We aren't in this for validation or friendship. This isn't about being loved or liked. This is about building something, and you have to have that mindset. You can't lose unless you give up."

There are critical techniques to use before, during, and after a business development meeting to improve resiliency. All of them rely on seeing rejection as temporary or external, rather than permanent or personal.

Pink described one critical technique we can use before an important meeting: using self-talk.[10] But this isn't the typical motivational speaker–style relentless focus on the positive. Social science suggests that the best self-talk is asking yourself a question, also known as *interrogative self-talk*. What this means is rather than saying "I can do it" like a mantra, ask questions such as "Can I do this?" as a better way to prepare for a tough meeting. Why? Because our natural instinct when we ask ourselves a question is to answer it. When we answer the question, we discover all the reasons how and why we really can do it.

An experiment that demonstrates the effectiveness of this technique was conducted by researchers from the University of Illinois and the University of Southern Mississippi. Two groups were asked to solve anagram puzzles, rearranging the letters in words to spell new words. Before they started, one group asked themselves whether they would solve the puzzles, while the other group told themselves they would solve the puzzle. The interrogative questioning group solved nearly 50 percent more puzzles.[11]

What about the client meeting itself? Here's where DCMi interviews showed a difference between Activator and non-Activators simply in the confidence they bring to a given interaction. Perhaps this is because they have more interactions overall or because they tend to bring more of a curious, questioning posture to those interactions, which gives them more information about why the client needs their services and the broader perspective that work will fit into. Demonstrating belief in your services is not only a good negotiation technique (which we will discuss in the next chapter) but is also important for early-stage business development.

When the meeting or interaction is completed, it is again a place where resilience is tested. Perhaps the meeting didn't quite go as planned or we've been rejected or deferred. Again, how we talk to ourselves in this moment has an outsized impact on our resiliency. It is easy to get discouraged or even start catastrophizing, especially if we've had a few rejections in a row. Research by Martin Seligman, a professor at the University of Pennsylvania and director of the University's Positive Psychology

Center, demonstrates that our explanatory style—the way we explain negative events—is a predictor of what he called "learned helplessness" or a propensity to give up easily.[12]

And the opposite is also true: an optimistic explanatory style helps resiliency. Seligman conducted research along with his colleague Peter Schulman with roughly one hundred sales agents at the Metropolitan Life Insurance Company and discovered that an optimistic explanatory style predicted how much they sold by a dramatic amount. Agents in the top decile sold 88 percent more insurance than those in the bottom decile. A pessimistic explanatory style, on the other hand, was a predictor of newly hired salespeople quitting within the first year. Those who scored on the pessimistic half of Seligman and Schulman's evaluation questionnaire would quit at twice the rate of optimistic salespeople.[13]

Like empathy, optimistic explanatory style is something that can be learned. At a minimum, we can tamp down our negative explanatory style as we encounter challenging situations or rejection. In his book *Learned Optimism*, Seligman suggests we ask ourselves three key questions. First, "Is this permanent?" More often than not, a rejection is temporary, and we need to shift our self-talk from "I'm terrible at this" to "I had a bad day. How do I get back on track?"[14] While Activators view a client *relationship* as permanent, they also recognize any given *interaction* with their important clients may not always go well. Asking if an outcome is permanent reminds us that we will have more opportunities to interact with a prospective client and that even the worst mistakes are surmountable with time; it also gets us in the mode of problem-solving how to reapproach the client in the future. One Activator explained that some of his best client relationships were forged as a result of a setback or hiccup early on:

> Nobody *tries* to make mistakes with their clients. But mistakes inevitably happen. It's how you rebound from those missteps that really determines whether this is going to be a one-time piece of work or a long-term relationship. I believe that deep down, my clients want to have a long-term relationship with me,

so I work hard to rebuild any lost trust to make sure we can move forward in a positive way. A lot of my colleagues feel like these moments are death blows to their client relationships and don't even try to recover from them.

The second question Seligman suggests we ask ourselves is "Is it pervasive?" This is an excellent question for broader reflection of the role a given interaction plays in our overall business strategy. Again, more often than not, a single interaction is a blip or aberration compared with our overall business development approach. But if it is indicative of a bigger issue in style or substance with a client, it presents an opportunity to look more clinically at the matter—and perhaps invite a colleague to join in and give feedback on the next interaction—rather than spiral into helplessness based on one rejection. "With any client, you've got to maintain an open mind toward adjusting the way you do things if you're at risk of damaging the relationship," one Activator told us, "but at the same time, you also need to know that there's a difference between a one-time slip-up and a systemic issue that you need to address. And clients know that too. Every mistake isn't a sign that your entire client engagement approach is broken."

The final—and perhaps most important—question Seligman recommends is, "Is it personal?" Most rejections in business development are not personal, but the reality is that most professionals take it personally. As buying groups increase in size and procurement or operations teams wield more influence over the purchase process, the influence of individual personality or style must, by necessity, decline. Of course, we can always lose the business by looking like we don't know how to work with our teammates, dominating the conversation, or missing critical cues from the client. But the number of times professionals attribute failure to something they did or didn't do is much higher than the percentage of time it's actually personal. By shifting our self-talk from "I screwed up" to "It wasn't the right time for this opportunity," we build our resiliency—and probably have a more accurate understanding of the real situation.

One participant in our training told a story along these lines. This partner at a law firm described how he happened to take the same train to London as a client that he was hoping to expand his work and relationship with, and they would often chat on the commute. One day, the partner asked the client if he wanted to go out to get a drink sometime, and the client demurred. Undaunted, he dropped it for a little while, and they kept occasionally meeting on the train. A few months later, he tried again a few times, but the client again turned him down. The partner started to think the client did not like him and the relationship was faltering. He would even start taking trains at different times to avoid the client—or he would move down the platform to avoid being in the same car. He began to feel awkward about their interactions.

Then, almost a year later, he happened to bump into the client at a coffee shop and decided to ask what was going on. "Hey, I don't mean to put you on the spot, but I've asked you a few times to go out for a drink," he said, "but it doesn't seem to work out. I can't help but wonder if maybe you're unhappy with something we've done?" The client was surprised by this and immediately put him at ease. "No, not at all! Your team has been great. It's just that I have a policy of not going out after work—that's my family time. Given my hectic work and travel schedule, I really can't disrupt that time." They arranged a regular lunch meeting that afternoon. They explored new ideas and new opportunities to work together, which resulted in a significant expansion of the business relationship.

By assuming it was personal, the partner wasted months of opportunity and anxiety over the client relationship when a simple, honest question fixed the issue and helped pave the way to a much broader partnership. And, even if it *was* personal and the client was only making up an excuse, an Activator knows that it doesn't help to internalize it. Activators understand that not every client is a good fit for them and that they are not going to convert opportunities with a one hundred percent success rate. Rather than wasting time obsessing about why a given client didn't appreciate their efforts or their engagement style, they quickly pivot to finding the next good-fit client who *will* appreciate their approach—and they know there are many more out there.

Roadblocks to Developing an Activator Mindset

As we've shown, the Activator approach is not reliant on personality: anyone can learn to be more of an Activator, and the three mindsets we've just covered should make it clear that these are learnable behaviors. But it turns out the average professional not only doesn't have these critical mindsets—but can often have a few traits that make developing new mindsets harder.

Take Dr. Larry Richard's work on law firm partners as an example. Richard, a trial lawyer who went on to get a doctorate in psychology, wondered whether there was a psychometric element that could explain why so many lawyers struggled with business development. He measured traits across more than thirty thousand lawyers in Am Law firms and found that while many possess traits that are quite helpful to the practice of law—like skepticism, abstract reasoning, and autonomy—lawyers tend to be much lower on average on three key attributes critical to effective business development: resilience (also called *ego-strength*), sociability, and cognitive empathy.[15] Richard found that the average lawyer enters the profession with lower-than-average strength in these key traits and, specifically, that 90 percent of lawyers score in the bottom half of the scale on resilience.

Sociability might not seem important, as it's often not seen as a "professional" posture. But it is in fact a key to successful connection. *Low sociability* means that one tends to keep away from the personal and stick to the formal in interactions. In practice, this means partners tend to stay away from authentic relationships in which they share personal details and vulnerabilities with clients. They thereby miss opportunities to learn similar details about those clients and, as a result, opportunities to build genuine relationships with them. Richard explains:

> You'll hear them call it "touchy-feely" and other disparaging things. But that's really unfortunate, because the science that's

emerging says that vulnerable, authentic connections are the single most important thing in producing all of the outcomes that human beings most dearly want in their lives. They produce high levels of life satisfaction, work satisfaction, and long-term relationship success—even longevity and good health. So, it's kind of a shame that lawyers treat it as a triviality but that's quite widespread.[16]

Simply put, for professionals looking to develop an Activator mindset, it's just as important to understand what to do as it is to understand the natural predispositions we each have that might stand in the way of progress. Doing this sort of self-assessment is arguably the first step in the journey.

Summary

Activators share three distinct mindsets that together lay a powerful foundation for their business development approach with clients. First, they are self-determined. They believe that they are in control of their own destiny when it comes to commercial outcomes. Their success isn't in the hands of clients, competitors, or market forces. Second, they are other-focused. They have cognitive empathy toward their clients. They understand the context surrounding the work they've been hired to do and understand their value drivers. They also have pride in their colleagues and don't shy away from making introductions and shifting the client's loyalty from "me" to "we." And third, they are highly resilient. They don't just bounce back quickly from setbacks but see setbacks as a unique opportunity to deepen their client relationships.

Mindset is different from personality. It is malleable and something that can be learned over time. Building an Activator mindset requires that professionals understand not just what mindsets to build but also what inherent traits one possesses that might inhibit optimal mindset development.

— 6 —

The Moments That Matter to an Activator

At every Activator training program we run around the world, we ask the attendees, "What is the one thing you most want to get out of the program?" The answers are surprisingly consistent: they want practical tips and tactics to keep business development moving, ideas for turning friends into clients, and to feel more confident in their business development efforts. This chapter unlocks many of those practical, tactical tips.

Want to be a better Activator? There are five clear pivot points when Activators distinguish themselves in the client engagement process: initial contact, opportunity creation, pitching, fee negotiation, and client setbacks. These day-to-day activities of business development will look familiar to most professionals: networking, making connections, building relationships, identifying and scoping the work, negotiating the contracts, and delivering the work. The difference, however, is in the details—specifically, the way the themes of committing, connecting, and creating come through in these moments for an Activator.

First, from a commitment standpoint, Activators are choosier about the moments they invest time in. For example, rather than spread themselves thinly across multiple events or occasions, Activators carefully curate the events they attend and are incredibly disciplined about getting the most out of the events they do attend. They also build a larger set of initial contacts than most and then prioritize and reprioritize them based on fit and responsiveness.

Second, when it comes to connecting, an Activator's success in these pivot points is powered by the network asset they've invested in. For example, on LinkedIn, Activators look for second-level connections and always use warm leads for introductions to those who match their ideal client profile. When it comes to events, Activators get access to attendee lists to preemptively contact attendees and schedule meetings. They also leverage their networks in other ways—for instance, securing invitations to join planning committees or to serve on panels. They then use their participation in panel discussions to give their contacts a chance to join in and build their own reputations. And rather than try to muscle through client setbacks on their own, Activators call on their network to support them, bringing the firm's broader capabilities to help right the ship.

Finally, Activator pivot points are infused with value creation. Activators are constantly thinking about how to deliver value—through insights about changes in the business or regulatory environment, connections to others in their networks, or just serving as a trusted sounding board in every client interaction. Insights, for instance, help them shift cocktail conversation at a client event from personal chitchat to business opportunities. Or they help generate relationships on LinkedIn when an Activator shares an insight in the comments of a target client's post. Or they form the basis of an email sent to an existing client that helps keep the relationship warm between paid engagements.

Across this chapter, we'll look closer at how Activator behaviors, habits, and mindsets fuse together for tactical success through every stage of the business development cycle.

Initial Contact

The most concentrated networking happens at events. Industry events—the more specialized the better—represent an incredible opportunity for precise targeting of new contacts, a chance to demonstrate expertise and share your take on industry changes and their implications, and a chance to deliver personal support to clients by getting them additional visibility or networking opportunities.

But Activators know that all events are not created equal and that there are highly leveraged and less leveraged ways to spend one's time at an event. In this section, we share a few of the event-related tactics we gleaned from our Activator interviews.

First, Activators advise that professionals prioritize events that are focused on a specific industry or subspecialty. One Activator lawyer, for example, told us he goes to an event focused on HVAC innovations every year for two reasons: "First, because it's been a specialty area of mine for a number of years, so these events are invaluable in terms of building and maintaining my network in the industry. And second, there are far fewer lawyers at these events than you'll find in other industry conferences."

Second, they advise that professionals consider joining an event committee. This is a great way for professionals to gain exposure and is much easier to accomplish at more specialized events. Committee members often get first dibs on speaking opportunities and are in a prime position to give speaking or panel opportunities to people in their networks. One other important but less well-known benefit: committee members typically get access to the full attendee list for an event, something that is normally reserved for top-tier sponsors. This gives them a leg up when it comes to prescheduling meetings with target clients and prospects in advance of the event. Activators recognize that attendees also want to ensure the event investment is worthwhile and typically welcome an invitation to meet for coffee or a quick connection before or after a session—particularly if the professional shares an insight that is relevant to the client's business.

Third, Activators advise setting goals for any event a professional attends. They have very clear targets in terms of how many meaningful interactions they'll have at an event. Based on some benchmarking we've done, we found that the typical Activator targets in the neighborhood of eight substantive interactions per day—a combination of prescheduled conversations with existing clients at an event and networking conversations with new contacts. "I figure that I'm at an event for a full business day—longer if you include breakfast beforehand and a cocktail reception or dinner afterward," one Activator told us, "Even when you take out a couple of hours for sessions you might attend or having to step out here and there for a client call, eight substantive interactions is my minimum to make an event worth the time investment."

Fourth, Activators recommend always "working the event." Activators—even introverted ones—don't clump with colleagues or stand around staring at their phones. They strike up conversations in elevators, in buffet lines, while on the organized morning run, and at cocktail hours. "My hardest workdays of the year are when I attend events. It's exhausting. But when I get back to my hotel room with a stack of new business cards or a bunch of new LinkedIn invitations to send, I know it's been worth it," one Activator told us.

Fifth, Activators say to follow up, follow up, and follow up some more. Even when the average professional manages to collect as many business cards or new LinkedIn connections as an Activator, the effort often goes to waste when they get sucked back into client work upon returning home. Activators recognize that a contact without follow-up is wasted and will quickly become stale. It is better to attend fewer events and take the time to establish relationships with the contacts met at those events than to attend many events, collecting stacks of business cards, and then not act on them.

Finally, Activators recommend reevaluating event value every year. Just because the firm is sponsoring an event or it feels like everyone will be there doesn't mean it makes sense for your platform. Although Activators may attend an event that is not valuable, they recognize that this is part of the learning process—as the saying goes, they won't get fooled again. "There's a big conference that everybody in my vertical seems to attend every year. But I went once and won't ever go back," one Activator shared with us. "There are too many attendees, too many competitor firms, and too many sessions. It's all too spread out. You can't find a table at a restaurant or a quiet coffee shop for a meeting all week. Give me a smaller, less showy event with opportunities for high-quality client engagement any day over the big shows." In addition, Activators are quick to spot when the pond is full of competitors and rarely waste time at those types of events.

Initial contact at live networking events

Even the most experienced professionals have revealed in training programs their dislike of a big cocktail party or networking event. A large room of strangers elicits a wide range of reactions from "waste of time" to "imposter syndrome." But with a basic script, even the most nervous, introverted professional can efficiently work a room. At the core of effective networking is genuine curiosity about the other person; it is also important to come equipped with a few observations or insights about the market to make an introduction with credibility and memorability.

An Activator networking conversation has six parts:

1. *Intro questions.* It's always better to start with questions about the person you're networking with rather than talk about yourself. Jim Collins, author of *Good to Great*, famously suggests the question "Where are you from?" as the perfect way to start any networking conversation. The spirit of the question is a great one, but in today's world, it is important to qualify it to ensure that you are not questioning whether someone "belongs" in the space—for instance, by modifying slightly to "Where did you fly in from?" or "Where is home for you?" or "Where is your company based?" The reason questions like these are so powerful is that they allow for immediate connections: you will likely find something in common with where they live or work that opens up the conversation for follow-on

questions. Even admitting you've never been to the other person's home city or state gives you something to talk about.

2. *Transition to business questions.* Opening questions like these often naturally segue to business. But if they don't, you'll need a way to shift the conversation more actively. Most likely you are meeting at an event with a speaker or theme; so, something like "What did you think of the points the keynote speaker was making?" or "I think we attended the same breakout session earlier. Is that an area your company is focused on right now?" creates a natural transition to business.

3. *Value delivery.* The shift to a business conversation gives you the right to introduce your business background at this point. Providing some background—what you do and how you have built up your expertise—should be combined with specific insights or observations about the field. Something like "I'd estimate that 80 percent of companies we work with fall into that trap" is a good example.

4. *The curiosity phase.* After sharing some insight and background, it's time to return to questions. The goal is to identify issues, challenges, or opportunities. "Is that anything you've experienced?" is a good way to turn back to the other person to validate your insight. "Interesting. Tell me more about that" is a good follow up. Regardless of the answer the client offers—whether it's "Yes, we've definitely experienced that!" or "No, can't say we've ever had that issue"—it opens up more surface area to explore.

5. *Securing the next step.* Here, channel your inner Activator and think about what would be most helpful to your new connection and offer it up: "Would it be helpful if . . . ?" is a great phrase here and can be followed by ". . . I connected you with my colleague who specializes in this area?" or ". . . I sent you some relevant material from our firm on this topic?" or ". . . we found some time to talk more about this?"

6. *The close.* Many early networkers struggle with how to get out of a conversation as much as how to get in. This can be much more straightforward than it seems, especially after the next step has been secured. "I don't want to monopolize your time. It was great to meet you, I'll follow up with a LinkedIn invitation (or email)" is a graceful way to bow out and move on to the next conversation.

Initial contact on LinkedIn

LinkedIn is one of the most important tools an Activator has at their disposal and nowhere is it more important than in the earliest stages of a client relationship when a new connection is engaged and brought into an Activator's network.

When we look at how professionals use LinkedIn, we see a few general patterns. First, we have the nonusers who are easy to identify in professional services: they are either not on the platform or they have a weak profile and presence with no profile photo, few connections, brief explanations of their expertise or prior experience, and no activity to speak of. It turns out this is pervasive in the professional services industry. In our training programs, we regularly encounter professionals who proudly proclaim they "don't do LinkedIn" or "don't see the value." Sometimes they don't maintain a LinkedIn presence because they don't believe their clients—in many cases, the most senior leaders of the biggest companies in the world—are even on the platform. In other cases, it's because they think LinkedIn is something only the firm's younger partners and associates use. And in many cases, it's because the professional believes themselves to be so well-known in their space that their biggest problem is not finding work but having too much inbound demand for their services—a problem they believe being on LinkedIn would only exacerbate.

The second pattern we see is influencers. Influencers are all about posting "one-to-many" content and collecting followers. They tend not to engage in content posted by others, nor do they send many outbound connection requests. They post their own content and then sit back and wait for the connection requests, direct messages, and followers to come in. Think of this approach as the digital equivalent to publishing a white paper or even putting up a billboard on the highway. These broadcasts are intended to send a signal to the market that the professional is a renowned thought leader in their particular space and, as a result, generate inbound demand for their services. Of the five profiles we identified in our research, the Expert profile is the most likely to use LinkedIn like an influencer.

The final pattern we see is the Activator pattern. Activators also post content, but their use of LinkedIn is more about one-to-one outreach, connection, and engagement than one-to-many broadcasting. Activators invest in making sure they have a compelling LinkedIn profile. They treat this as the anchor point from which they build out their networks. Unlike an influencer, however, an Activator is less concerned about developing a personal brand. DCMi UK managing director Alex Low is a noted LinkedIn expert who has trained thousands of professionals on the ins and outs of using the platform for client development. As he explains,

> Activators don't believe that any client will choose to work with them or not because of their incredible LinkedIn profiles. It is, however, important to bear in mind that if you are creating or publishing content [that] leads your intended audience to your profile, it makes sense to back it up. This is no different from a website, and this is how you should treat your profile on LinkedIn. Your profile is a website that is about you and what you can do for your clients, so you want it to reflect this. If you search your name in search engines, your LinkedIn profile is usually the first thing that comes up.

Practically speaking, Activator LinkedIn profiles always have a banner image (sometimes something personal but more often a banner provided by their company's marketing or social media team), an up-to-date profile picture, and a compelling headline. We see many different approaches to headlines taken by Activators. Some just list their titles, some list their area of expertise or industry focus, and some take a more descriptive approach, highlighting the attributes they believe set them apart in the market—for instance, "Innovative legal problem-solver helping life sciences companies protect their intellectual property." Activators who take this last approach tell us that they will ask their best clients how they would describe them and use that language to craft their headline.

Similarly, in the "About" section, we see Activators using this real estate in many different ways. Low explains that "there is no right or wrong way to compose this section of your profile; however, the best Activators think about it as the way they would describe themselves to their next client, not their next job." And finally, there is the "Experience" section. If a professional uses their CV or personal experience to pitch themselves to a client, the experience section of their LinkedIn profile should match that. And, of course, professionals should make sure their other credentials—education, publications, certifications, and skills—are complete and up to date. In our experience, Activators are much more likely to have client recommendations than influencers and, of course, nonusers.

With a compelling profile in hand, Activators then focus on building and activating their networks. As Low explains, "Every professional has influence. What they need to consider is how they can use this in a meaningful way to move their message through their network of influence in order to get to new people." Of course, Activators *do* have larger LinkedIn networks than non-Activators. But it's important to remember that Activator networks are typically in the three thousand range. Professionals who have tens of thousands of connections are more likely taking an influencer approach than an Activator approach.

Activators tend to define their LinkedIn networks more broadly than most. They consider not just their first-tier connections, but their second-tier connections as well. Low illustrates using his own network as an example:

> Let's say I'm trying to position myself and my firm to financial services CMOs in the UK and, to do that, I want to broaden my network to include more of these types of buyers. I have nearly a

thousand second-tier connections that fit that description. That means I can get a potential introduction to a thousand new opportunities. This also means that if I were to post something aimed at CMOs in the financial services space, and I have an engaged network of first-degree CMO connections, I can potentially influence a further thousand CMOs toward me.

One of the hacks Activators use to grow their first-tier connections is to leverage their colleagues to get warm introductions to potential new clients. This is one of the reasons an Activator's network includes a robust number of internal colleagues, not just outside connections.

Low says Activators "think of LinkedIn as the biggest conference in the world." They are extremely intentional about how they engage. As our research and LinkedIn's own analysis shows, they tend to do this multiple times per day, though typically in small one- to two-minute increments, and often between client calls or while walking to grab lunch. Activators are far more likely to follow the companies they work with as well as those they would like to work with. They also follow the C-suite of their clients' organizations. The reason for this, Low explains, is that once a company or executive is followed, the user will see that company or leader's posts in their feed and will have visibility into the issues, topics, and opportunities they care about. Much of this will be work-related content, but increasingly, users are posting more personal information that gives an Activator visibility into the causes a client cares about or perhaps a personal struggle they're dealing with, both of which represent great opportunities to deliver value at a personal level.

Activators are also much more purposeful in how they engage their network—both their first and second-tier connections as well as the companies and leaders they follow. They do this in a few ways. First, they like and comment on posts that important connections make as well as those of prospective connections that fit their ideal client profile. Second, they make a point to comment on discussion threads where they can showcase their expertise, experience, perspectives, and insights. All of this is done for one of two reasons: either to maintain, deepen, or "validate" an existing relationship with a client or to pave the way for a new connection. "It's critical for professionals to understand how LinkedIn works," Low explains, "In short, every action has a reaction. Therefore, every like, comment, message, recent connection acceptance, or follow will trigger the algorithm to show you more of that content. The same goes for when people engage with you and your content. When you engage on the platform and your audience engages, you are creating lots of ripples in the system, moving your brand and content through your network."

Activators recognize that engaging in targeted conversations where second-level connections may join in is more powerful than posting a piece of content and hoping it gets seen in a person's feed. They do post content, but they spend more time engaging in conversation by commenting on other peoples' posts. We heard countless stories from Activators about how a big piece of work or a new client started with a like or comment on a LinkedIn post.

One important point about an Activator's use of LinkedIn: they are not selling their services directly to clients on the platform. Instead, as Low says, their LinkedIn activity is decidedly about "creating the shortest route to a conversation with someone—where they and the client believe there is an opportunity to solve a business challenge together." Put differently, while they are indeed very active on the platform, their goal is to move the conversation off LinkedIn and into another channel. One Activator shared an example of this with us:

> I use it when I'm going to town for a conference and I'll send messages on LinkedIn saying, "I'll be in town, let me know if you want to connect." Recently, I was going to be in Minneapolis. So I went into LinkedIn and asked, "Who do I know in Minneapolis, and who would I like to spend some time with?" I created a small dinner event, inviting some target clients. One person got back to me and said she couldn't make it, but a member of her team would love to come. That person came to the dinner and then he asked us to visit them at their headquarters the very next day. They've been a client ever since.

Opportunity Creation

Activators create opportunities by bringing insight to clients and generating value in between paid work or when engaging prospective clients. Even if a client doesn't bite on a new insight floated by an Activator, the simple fact that they are making the effort to think one step ahead for the client helps to keep them top of mind and in the consideration set should a need arise in the client's world.

One Activator told us that when thinking about clients, he always asks himself, "What do I think the client should be worried about six months, two years down the line? And how can we get ahead of that for them?" As we've discussed, this sort of insight delivery is a central element to how Activators create value for clients and surface new opportunities for paid work.

Delivering insights to clients should follow a general four-step flow (see figure 6-1). For the purposes of illustration, consider the example of a multidisciplinary consulting firm trying to engage customer service executives in the banking sector on AI transformation work. The typical outreach would sound something like this: "We're one of the leading AI transformation consultancies in the world and have partnered with numerous leading banks to drive new efficiencies and customer experience gains in their service centers. We would love to meet with you to tell you more about our experience in this area and see if there is an opportunity to support you and your organization on this front." It's a classic features and benefits-led pitch.

An insight-based outreach is different in four key respects. First, it starts with a *hypothesis* about what the professional thinks is weighing on the client's mind. Clients, it turns out, intensely dislike when professionals ask them what's keeping them up at night—which, ironically, most professionals think is a great way to be client-centric. Clients report to us that this sort of open-ended questioning is overused by professionals to the point that it's become exhausting for clients to have to tell every professional they meet their top priorities and challenges. Instead,

FIGURE 6-1

A framework for insights to create client opportunities

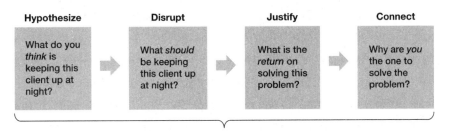

Hypothesize	Disrupt	Justify	Connect
What do you *think* is keeping this client up at night?	What *should* be keeping this client up at night?	What is the *return* on solving this problem?	Why are *you* the one to solve the problem?

Insight-based messages follow a distinct structure and flow, leading to what makes the service provider's value proposition unique.

clients appreciate when a professional approaches them with a hypothesis informed by what other clients are wrestling with. A simple hypothesis-based opener—for instance, "I'm sure you're similar to most of our clients in the banking sector who are focused on how AI can drive greater efficiencies in customer service delivery"—immediately distinguishes the professional from others in the market because it signals that the discussion will be client-focused rather than focused on the professional or firm's capabilities.

The second step in an insight-based message is to *disrupt* how the client is thinking about the issue right now. This is often positioned as a "Did you know . . . ?" component of the message. For instance, "What we've found in our work in this area is that leaders need to bring their frontline teams along and help them see AI as a powerful ally to them rather than a threat, and that a disengaged team is the fastest way to derail any AI transformation project." A tip for professionals struggling to identify a disruptive angle to their message is to ask the question, "What is the one thing I *wish* all of my clients appreciated about this threat or opportunity that most of them overlook, underestimate, or are altogether unaware of?" The key is to remember that this is your opportunity to get the client to think about their own needs, risks, or opportunities in a different way.

Third, professionals should *justify* their claim. For example, "When these teams are not engaged in the AI journey, it can lead to technology investments failing to generate their intended ROI and, worse, lower discretionary effort and higher intent to leave among frontline employees. In our analysis, we've found that banks that engage their front line early on in AI transformation efforts generate twice the return and half of the disengagement of banks that do not." One piece of advice we can give professionals here is to focus less on the ROI of working with you (which, of course, requires the client to buy your services since you are a part of that return equation) and instead focus on what *The Challenger Sale* authors call ROPE, or *return on pain eliminated*, which is more supplier-agnostic and instead articulates to the client the benefit they will capture by successfully addressing a threat or opportunity, regardless of who they hire to do the work.[1]

And, finally, the message should *connect* to the professional or firm's unique differentiators. "As the only consultancy that combines AI deployment expertise with human capital expertise, we're uniquely positioned to navigate these difficult transformation obstacles. I'd love to grab some time to share our point of view on this topic and tell you a bit more about some of the work we've been doing with peer organizations in this space."

Pitching

The pitch, whether an informal call to confirm work or a formal presentation in response to an RFP, is a distillation of all the value and relationship conversations that came before it. It's also a moment that illustrates the Activator principles of committing, connecting, and creating most clearly. While our study revealed that Activators don't spend more time on pitching than other profiles (18 percent of business development time for Activators versus 20 percent for other profiles), many of the activities they do within and around the pitch are quite different than the other profiles.

Activators enter a pitch better positioned than their peers because they stay connected to prospective clients. By leveraging their networks to provide value between paid work, they are better positioned to *shape* the pitch, not just to be in contention for the work. Having conversations before the buying group is formed and equipping decision-makers with criteria that help them make good decisions—decisions that lead back to a professional or firm's unique strengths—all position an Activator in an advantageous way before the pitch even happens.

What's more, as we've noted, we know that clients today are at least 60 percent of the way through the purchase journey before they engage professionals or firms directly. Engaging in value-filled interactions before a pitch helps an Activator to be choosy about opportunities before time-consuming pitch deck creation and rehearsal need to happen. It is a common belief among junior professionals that they can start with commodity work and build up to more strategic work, but this approach does not typically pan out and ends up taking quite a bit of time away from better opportunities that are more worthy of a professional's time.

Activators also handle the pitch moment itself very differently. In our training programs, we hear a lot of stories about pitches gone wrong: the occasion where a professional introduced himself to others on his own team during the pitch; the time when a senior partner on a Zoom call kept talking for ten minutes after being disconnected; the time when one practice group leader spoke for fifty-five minutes of an hourlong pitch and didn't give anybody else on the team a chance to even say hello. While you'd think such obvious disasters could have been avoided, they are a reminder that even the best firms and the best professionals can fall into these traps.

At a high level, there are four key elements to an Activator pitch:

- *Understanding the audience.* Activators know that their pitch messages must be highly tailored and targeted. They don't roll out the standard "firm-practice-team" pitch deck loaded with background and credentials up front.

- *Differentiation through insight.* Activators are keenly aware of the exact ways in which their capabilities are different from those of their competitors, but they don't lead with those points. Instead, they lead with insights into threats or opportunities clients face, helping them to see around the corner in a way that connects with their unique capabilities.

- *Proof points.* Activators back up their insights with specific data and examples that demonstrate the success they have had with other clients, and they come equipped with client success stories. They know that claims of unique, differentiated capabilities are only warranted if they can be credibly demonstrated.

- *Two-way learning and team-based delivery.* Activators ensure that the pitch is not a presentation; through rigorous rehearsal and confirmation of roles everyone will play in a group pitch, they ensure that the team's points are delivered succinctly and that they personally avoid dominating the discussion. Throughout the pitch, Activators also ask multiple questions to ensure the client is tracking and receiving the value they expected.

Many of those themes describe a great pitch no matter what type of professional is delivering it, but there are specific components that embody the Activator principles of committing and creating.

Committing to preparation

Activators never deliver a pitch without holding a pre-pitch call with the client. Too often, professionals head into pitch meetings with incomplete information and misaligned expectations; this is not the case with Activators.

The pre-call is a brief phone call with a client that takes place before the pitch—ideally, a week or so in advance. There are three simple agenda items: to understand last-minute dynamics, confirm attendees and agenda, and set the tone. This call allows an Activator to ensure the right people are going to be in the room, understand if anything has changed, and convey excitement and commitment about the opportunity. The language is as basic as, "I know we have already connected, but things change. To make sure we're making the best use of everyone's time, I wanted to grab fifteen minutes just to go over agenda, attendees, and expectations."

But more than how it works, it's what it does. Activators tell us that there are three benefits to a pre-pitch call:

- *Avoiding wasted time.* It's better to learn in advance that the call is not well set up so that it can be rescheduled or even canceled. There's nothing worse than assembling a pitch team and rehearsing the pitch only to discover that a large portion of the client team could not make it or were not brought into the discussion.

- *Getting critical signals.* Is it impossible to get the pre-call scheduled? Can't get the key contact on the phone? These signals are huge red flags for Activators. If a client is unwilling to engage in a pre-pitch call, most Activators quickly conclude that they are not as well positioned for this work as they thought or are just being used as a foil for a preferred provider. Of course, sometimes there are procurement rules requiring that no supplier have an advantage in advance of a pitch; but aside from those unique scenarios, a prospective client's unwillingness to invest time is a strong signal about a professional's ultimate chances of success in the pitch.

  One Activator in a talent advisory firm mentioned that, for clients with whom he has a good relationship, one question he will ask on a pre-call is, "Is there a level playing field for this work?" This question works well on multiple levels. Ideally, the prospect answers honestly and gives useful information about the opportunity. But, even if they don't, if they insist it is indeed a level playing field, they will be that much more inclined to make it so in practice. As Robert Cialdini has shown in his research on the components of influence, humans have a strong instinct for consistency in what they say and do, especially in response to small and reasonable requests they agree to.[2]

- *Looking "sponsored" in the meeting itself.* After Activators have used the pre-call to confirm the agenda, they can start the meeting sounding like an insider—as part of the team: "In our conversation yesterday, [client contact] mentioned that the best use of our time today would be to cover X, Y, and Z. Does everyone agree?"

Creating peak moments

Another differentiator for Activators during pitches is an understanding of how to create value through "peak moments" in a pitch. Anyone who has been on the receiving side of a series of competitive pitches understands that the true challenge is remembering which firm said what after the pitches are done. Activators therefore optimize for memorability. In their book *The Power of Moments*, Chip and Dan Heath looked into what parts of experiences we remember. Typically, they found, people remember the best or worst parts of an experience—or the last part of the experience. They then looked deeper at what made for those "best moments" and discovered four characteristics: elevation (of senses, stakes, surprise), insight, pride, or connection (especially through moments of shared meaning).[3]

For Activators, this appears first and foremost in the use of insights. Delivered well, an insight elevates the stakes, surprises through the disruption of assumptions, and creates a great opportunity for a peak moment in the pitch. The added benefit of using insights in pitches is that the insight can stand alone as a gift of value to the other party. At the end of a pitch, Activators often say something like "No matter who you choose to work with, we encourage you to use this approach." In addition to being a demonstration of the kind of value Activators will demonstrate throughout any engagement, it's also a way to display generosity and selflessness—attributes desired in any professional.

There are other peaks that Activators engineer as well. For example, in one interview, an Activator attorney shared how he staged an argument with another member of his team in the middle of the pitch. As the argument continued, it became clear these were the points they would make in court and showed how compellingly they could make them. Another told us how, when they were pitching to a retail client, everyone in the introduction talked about their connection to the client's product. A consulting firm shared how they did a photo shoot for a particularly important retail client where the pitching team wore the client organization's store associate uniforms. In the pitch, the firm didn't say anything about the pictures, just scattered them throughout the deck. The first comment they received from the client: "Tell us more about those photos!" And another Activator told us that she always tries to create a memorable moment for clients by suggesting they take their phones out to take a picture of a key slide or dog-ear a specific page in their pitch deck for later reference.

Fee Negotiation

Discussing fees and budgets can be one of the hardest parts of being a professional. While many professionals go to graduate schools that include negotiation classes where they learn concepts like ZOPA (the zone of potential agreement) or BATNA (the best alternative to a negotiated agreement), in practice the changes in client buying behavior we have seen in recent years make negotiation much more challenging.[4]

The disaggregation of services, the involvement of procurement in evaluating service providers, and the formalization of purchasing processes are all designed to increase the power of the buyer in any negotiation. There are many documented examples of the value of power in negotiation. As Harvard's Program on Negotiation states, "The powerful are also more persistent than other negotiators, less likely to give up when confronted with setbacks and obstacles, and more likely to strive toward more aggressive goals."[5]

Here is where the Activator mindsets of being other-focused, self-determined, and resilient play a key role. By being other-focused, Activators increase overall value by understanding what would add value to any fee negotiation. By being self-determined, Activators recognize the control they have over the outcomes and bring confidence to the negotiation—leveling out the playing field because they recognize that *perceived* power is as important as *actual* power in a negotiation. And by being resilient, Activators stick with the negotiation long enough to find creative solutions that bring more value to both parties.

Expanding the field of negotiables

An Activator recognizes that while the client may run right at price, there are many more negotiables that they can leverage to get to a successful outcome. When buying a car or a house, at the end of the negotiation there is typically an exchange of money for goods; while services can be offered, they typically pale in comparison to the value of the asset itself. But with professional services, there are innumerable variables in play: the scope of the engagement, the makeup of the team, the timeline, additional services that may be adjacent to the core scope of the work, the professional's willingness to customize a solution for a client—and many more.

Negotiation experts refer to this type of negotiation as *integrative*, as compared to *distributive* negotiation, where both parties see negotiables as fixed and work to maximize the size of their personal slice of the pie.[6] There's plenty of room for added value for all parties involved in a negotiation for professional services work, and Activators' perspective-taking, resilience, and confidence allows them to creatively explore outcomes that maximize this value. Moreover, these Activator mindsets are helpful beyond the actual fee negotiation phase of a new client engagement; they are crucial during moments of expectation management and clarifying and communicating value relative to the engagement's cost or the number of billable hours.

Activators do not feel like they are born negotiators, but rather that they are *prepared* negotiators. One Activator told us that he always makes a list of potential negotiables: from things that are easy to give away (e.g., arranging a free conversation with a colleague on an issue that is adjacent to the paid work) to things that are more difficult to give away (i.e., price or critical terms and conditions): "You should always come to a negotiation with a game plan. Clients will always start any negotiation by saying your rates are too high and will ask for a price concession. This should be the last thing you capitulate on—there are many things you can do to enhance the value of the work for the client that are cheaper for you and your firm to deliver and, candidly, will deliver a lot more value to the client than a discount."

Being other-focused in negotiations

A big part of an Activator's effectiveness in negotiations stems from their desire to deeply understand where the client is coming from. As one Activator told us,

> Every client will ask for a discount and want to negotiate down our fees. But the reason they ask . . . varies dramatically, one client to the next. Some are under real budget pressure, some are actually bonused on keeping spend below certain thresholds, and some are just trying to look like a hero to the higher-ups in the organization. You need to understand what's driving the client's request. Once you know what's behind their request, you'll find there are a lot more tools at your disposal than just lowering your fees.

Perspective-taking and empathy in negotiations were explored deeply by researchers Adam Galinsky, William Maddux, Debra Gilin, and Judith White. Across three studies, they found that cognitive perspective-taking increased an individual's ability to discover hidden agreements and to both create and claim resources at the bargaining table. Perspective-taking promotes trust between negotiators by helping them overcome suspicious assumptions about each other's behavior.[7]

To assist in this, Activators are very explicit in confirming their understanding during negotiations or budget discussions. These are phrases commonly used by Activators:

- "Do you mind if I ask how you are feeling about this?" when it is not clear how things are progressing

- "What have you done in the past that has worked at this stage?" when negotiations feel like they've reached an impasse

- "I want to make sure I really understand your situation" when alignment is challenging

Having confidence in one's own power

Activators are self-determined and believe that they are in control of their business development outcomes. In negotiations, this appears as a recognition of their own power and ability to walk away when the situation calls for it.

Most of the recent changes in client buying behavior in the professional services market have been made with the intent to increase the client's power, particularly in pitches and negotiations. But just because the client has taken action to increase power in a negotiation doesn't mean they actually *feel* like they have power. During the heyday of procurement's rise in B2B purchasing, BayGroup International surveyed sales reps and procurement officers to understand who was perceived to have more power in negotiations. The results revealed that while 75 percent of reps believe that procurement has the upper hand in the rep-customer relationship, 75 percent of procurement officers believe that sales reps have more power.[8] Given this difference in perceived power, it's crucial for professionals to adopt a mindset of self-determination and not dupe themselves into believing that they are going to be on the losing end of a negotiation before it even begins.

When both sides perceive similar levels of power, they tend to be more open about what they are looking for and more creative in finding solutions. As long as they have something to gain, high-power negotiators typically will be more persistent than other negotiators.[9] Researchers Rebecca Wolfe and Kathleen McGinn found that "negotiating pairs who perceived a smaller difference in relative power reached agreements of greater integrativeness than pairs who perceived a greater power difference, even after controlling for alternatives and aspirations."[10]

What does this look like in practice? There are a few best practices we see among confident Activators. The first is perhaps the most controversial: Activators do not offer price first. The moment when a professional is asked "How much will it cost?" is always fraught. Research shows that when the price range is generally well known, it is an advantage to go first and anchor on a high number. Psychologists Amos Tversky and Daniel Kahneman documented the concept of *anchor bias*, whereby we are strongly influenced by numbers presented to us initially. In one study, researchers showed a group of study participants a set of random numbers and then asked them a series of questions—for instance "What is the percentage of United Nation countries in Africa?"—and, as irrational as it might seem, the majority of participants' responses were based on the random numbers they had been shown before the questions were asked.[11]

But in professional services, the range of prices tends to be wide, so it is better to get information before putting price on the table. Harvard's Program on Negotiation also recognizes that, "When a commodity is unique or offers special value to certain bidders, sellers may ... see an advantage in allowing buyers to bid first."[12] It is precisely the uniqueness of most professional services that makes it an advantage to go second and learn about the buyer's budget or expectations before offering a price. Asked to give a price range by the client, an Activator will typically respond with "Well, there are a number of variables involved here. Can you give me a sense of the budget you are working with?"

Activators' confidence shows up even more clearly in the next step: rather than offering a specific price, they offer a price *range* in which the low point is the price they actually want—a tactic recommended by Chris Voss in his book, *Never Split the Difference*.[13] One Activator told us that she tries not to box herself in with specific prices and instead tends to say something along the lines of, "Even though we probably need to confirm a few things, what we have typically seen when working with other clients is a fee range between $75,000 and $100,000." Activators realize that once you have the initial information about budget and know that you are in the right ballpark, you are well positioned to maximize the value of an agreement—especially if it is anchored using a range in the way Voss recommends.

There is one more component of this positioning that makes it so effective: by referencing what other clients have paid, an Activator is able to leverage a powerful psychological effect known as *social proof.* Robert Cialdini and his colleagues illustrate this concept with a particularly compelling example from an infomercial writer named Colleen Szot. Her standard approach to get people to order products seen on TV was to say, "Operators are waiting; please call now." Then Szot changed just a few words of the line so that it read, "If operators are busy, please call again," and calls skyrocketed.[14] As Cialdini explains, with the new words "you're probably imagining operators going from phone call to phone call without a break. After all, if the phone lines are busy, then other people like me who are also watching this infomercial are calling too."[15]

The final piece of self-determination in Activator negotiations: they don't discount rates initially. A 2023 law department benchmarking survey conducted by the Association of Corporate Counsel found that, on average, 83 percent of clients use discounted hourly rates. As a result, many lawyers assume their counterparts are aware that discounts are available and start with a discounted rate. But this misses the opportunity to frame the discount. Instead, an Activator negotiation sounds like this: "We are always open to discussion around rates, especially for this type of work and with important clients that we would like to build a long-term relationship with, but here is our rate card." Even if the work is most likely to get discounted in the future, this ensures that the discount is in exchange for an understanding that this is an unusual circumstance or long-term relationship. It also leaves open the possibility to time-box the discount. For example, "How about we discount our rates for the first three months until you are able to gauge the quality of our work?"

Getting creative and preserving the relationship

An Activator's resilience is one of their strongest tools in a negotiation. Resilient and confident negotiators get more creative with options to increase the integrative value of the negotiation—increasing the total pie, rather than just their individual slice.

The basis for an Activator's creative, integrative negotiations begins with a deep understanding of all of the sources of value they can deliver to the client. This gives Activators critical information both for the initial proposal and for later trade-offs that may be necessary when getting to fee alignment. And once this information is gathered, Activators will follow a natural order in getting to fee alignment, to ensure they maximize value during a negotiation without giving up too much.

If there is a struggle to reach fee alignment, the Activator's first step is to add value rather than to discount. More often than not, they offer ideas for supporting the client's personal objectives. This might sound like: "Your budget constraints seem significant, but we are not able to discount any further. Would it help if I found additional ways to add value outside of the fees; for example, off-the-clock time with one of our experts on that other issue you mentioned to me?" Harvard's negotiation program points out the value of this strategy as well; a good strategy for integrative negotiations is to "give your counterpart a gift," especially if it is labeled as a concession and highlights the sacrifices being made. Similarly, Tversky and Kahneman's research shows that people in negotiations prefer multiple small gains over single equivalent large gains, so these should be given out individually and framed as multiple discrete concessions.[16]

If alignment is still not found, Activators move on to "stage two" negotiations: confining discounts and aiming for concessions in return. This can seem like classic quid pro quo but it should be delivered with empathy. It's not, "I'll do this if you'll do that." The concession should be something reasonable and fair to the client—for example, a commitment that there is a time limit to the discount. "I can tell this is an important issue to you and we don't want to lose you as a client. It's going to be hard to get to this number because our rates are fixed by my firm. But if I could get us there, I will need a commitment from you that this pricing is only good for this piece of work. Is that fair? Can you make that commitment?" Again, the commitment language is particularly powerful because it calls on another one of Cialdini's principles of influence: commitment and consistency. When individuals make a public commitment to something, they are much more likely to follow through on it.[17] "What else do you need to make this work?" can be a good phrase to prevent unexpected items from coming up later. If they give you a list of items, they're effectively committing that there's nothing else that they will need beyond that.

A 1983 study published in the *Personality and Social Psychology Bulletin* showed the power of commitment. In the first phase of the study, researcher Joseph Schwarzwald and his team asked half the residents of an apartment building to sign a petition for the establishment of a social club for the disabled. For the second stage two weeks later, they asked all residents to donate, even those who had not been asked to sign the petition. According to the study, 92 percent of those who had signed the petition donated, compared with just over 50 percent of those who had not been asked to sign it.[18]

The final stage for Activators struggling to get to fee alignment is to wait. Most professionals tend to be overeager to get a piece of client business over the line; they've put so much effort into the negotiations and it feels so tempting to just make those last few concessions so that the agreement can be signed and the work can start. But because they are other-focused, Activators remember that the client has also put in just as much work and energy—and that they are likely just as eager to get the work started. With the passage of time, counterparts have a moment to think through other creative options and to reduce the emotions in the negotiation.

There is one final phrase we heard from Activators generally, but particularly when it comes to negotiations: "Is this fair?"—a question that

Chris Voss recommends.[19] Activators recognize that above any given engagement or matter, the relationship with the client is much more important in the long run. Fairness to both sides is something that everyone can agree is desirable and can both jolt the client out of any distributive negotiation mindset they may be in but, more importantly, can serve to remind them that everybody's intentions are good. In a tough or high-stakes moment, the phrase "Is this fair?" can defuse the tension remarkably well.

Client Setbacks

The final pivot point for Activators is in how they handle client setbacks. As much as we wish they wouldn't happen, issues or friction or differences in expectations arise all the time in professional services. Overall, Activators treat these moments with honesty and speed—and quickly work to rebuild trust once a setback happens.

There's a phenomenon in customer service called the *service recovery paradox*, which refers to the fact that a customer's loyalty to a company often *increases* after a service failure, provided the company effectively resolves the issue. This effect hinges on the company's ability to respond quickly, empathetically, and effectively to resolve the problem.[20] This is not to say that one should welcome or create issues—just that, when they happen, Activators swarm the problem immediately and work hard to rebuild trust, which often makes the relationship stronger than it was before.

Research shows that rebuilding trust is easier when the initial basis of trust is strong. As researchers Roy Lewicki and Carolyn Wiethoff explain, "Relationships characterized by calculus-based or identification-based distrust are likely to be conflict-laden, and eruption of conflict within that relationship is likely to feed and encourage further distrust. . . . Once such negative expectations are created, actions by the other become negative self-fulfilling prophecies."[21] The basis of trust Activators build with their clients, therefore, is a minimum requirement to effectively handle setbacks.

Activators also recognize the easy confusion between budget and value. In professional services, most firms find that budget and perceived value are highly correlated. If clients feel as though they got the value their budget allows for, they will be satisfied and more loyal. If they feel as though the value derived is not equal to the current budget, disagreement and disloyalty are likely to ensue. For this reason, Activators communicate frequently about both budget and value with their clients. And since perceived value can decay over time, Activators will remind clients of past value and make sure to deliver additional value when facing impending renewals, budget conversations, or negotiations.

Handling a "No thanks"

There is one additional setback moment in which Activators distinguish themselves: after losing a pitch or piece of work.

What is the Activator way to handle a "No thanks?" Activators tell us that they always check their assumptions and dig deeper to make sure they *are* being rejected. If a prospective client says "Of course, I would never use you guys for that," is that clearly a "no" or is it something else?

Average business developers tend to say "Thank you for that feedback" and take a client comment like this as a rejection. Activators, however, move quickly into discovery mode. They will ask questions that help them to understand what the client is really saying before assuming it is a rejection. All of this is done with sensitivity, of course. Activators don't pressure the client into changing their minds, but it is nevertheless critical to understand what's behind statements like these. Perhaps the client is unaware of your firm's capabilities, or perhaps they believe you wouldn't entertain a particular kind of work given your rate card? Sensitive questioning allows Activators to push back against assumptions the client may have while potentially gathering information about other firms the client works with and the broader business objectives they can be supporting beyond the immediate opportunity they were trying to create.

Bouncing back from bad meetings

Let's take a more straightforward example of potential rejection and the opportunity for resiliency: when a professional has a bad meeting. Imagine the moment after leaving a meeting when a professional has the strong sense that it did not go well. Perhaps they just didn't click with the client or their team, perhaps there was an error of some kind in their pitch materials or in how they responded to the client's questions, or perhaps there was some awkwardness when they didn't get the responses they expected.

As Martin Seligman reminds us, professionals need to manage their self-talk in that instance; it's not permanent, nor is it pervasive or personal. This gives an Activator the energy to do what is most important: preserve the relationship. After a bad meeting, most Activators typically wait a day or so before looping back and engaging the client in an open discussion. They seek to learn a little about follow-ups from the meeting and to gauge the client's demeanor. Activators must demonstrate ownership up front: "I would love to hear your thoughts, but I am not sure you really got a whole lot of value out of that meeting. It felt to me it was not the best discussion and likely not the best use of your team's time." That gives the client permission to share their thoughts candidly without hurting the relationship.

Once an Activator has gotten critical information and aired any concerns about the meeting, they offer something of value to make sure the conversation is not simply for gathering feedback. Perhaps they share some data, research, or other insights that would be helpful to them: "I did want to share this—I thought it might be interesting to you." Or perhaps they offer to help with something to demonstrate that they are still willing to invest in the relationship; for example, a connection that would be helpful to the client or some support for their team.

It's clear how this mindset and conversation accomplish several goals and are the opposite of the learned helplessness many professionals exhibit when it comes to business development. They preserve the relationship, demonstrate what it's like to work with the professional as a service provider and, most importantly, show that the professional has a posture of curiosity and a willingness to accept feedback, thereby setting up occasions for further interactions that will provide the opportunity to mend whatever issues arose.

The loss call

The hardest "no" of all comes after losing a pitch. At a minimum, a pitch entails several hours of prep and presentation but, in many cases, it likely took dozens of hours of coordination and rehearsals across multiple departments, especially for big pitches. And when the call comes that the client has selected a different firm, it can be devastating. But this is the moment, perhaps above any other, when Activators distinguish themselves.

Once that call or email comes in, we tend to see two typical responses. The first is to move on. In some ways, this is healthy—after all, it can be easy to catastrophize a lost opportunity, and moving on feels like a resilient response in this situation. The second response we see is for the professional to reach out to the client to ask for feedback as to why they weren't selected for the work.[22]

Activators know that both of these approaches miss an important opportunity. Activators engage in what is called a "loss call"—a moment that capitalizes on one more of Cialdini's principles of influence: reciprocity.[23] While most people understand that acts of kindness are often repaid with kindness, they often underestimate exactly how strong this instinct is. This was well illustrated by a 2002 research study that looked at restaurant tipping. After measuring the baseline level of tips given by diners, the researchers found that the average tip increased by 3 percent when a single candy was given with the bill. Next, they instructed the waitstaff to offer two candies, and this led to a 14 percent increase in tips. For the final experiment, the waitstaff would give one candy, walk away from the table, then double back and offer another candy. This led to a 23 percent increase in tips.[24]

Psychologists explain this by stressing that humans simply hate to feel indebted to others. Activators use this concept during loss calls to protect the relationship and set the stage for future work.

The call has a very simple structure:

1. *"We're disappointed, of course, but we know these decisions can be difficult and completely respect it."* This signals that you understand and are not reopening the discussion, defusing some of the potential conflict they may worry about.

2. *"We would love to get your feedback as to where we were strong and where we fell short"* or *"Do you have any advice for how we might approach future opportunities to be more successful?"* This shows you are open to feedback and demonstrates how you like to work. And you might get some helpful feedback in the process.

3. *"We really enjoyed getting to know you, the team, and the company."* This is the bridge to show this was personal and not just business.

4. *"I would like to offer up my support and thought this [insight, connection, other offer] would be helpful to have as you and your team embark on this work."* This is the key piece. Offering some help on the issue serves several purposes. First, it demonstrates generosity; second, it shows an understanding of the issues at hand and what help might be needed; and third, it gives the client an occasion to keep talking to you.

When we talk about the importance of loss calls in our Activator training sessions, participants have validated its success and expressed how—if they offer something helpful even after losing the business opportunity—they often get the somewhat sheepish call a few months later: "Well, as you know, we went with your competitor, but we're off to a rocky start. Could you come and spend some time with us? We would like to pick your brain a bit and perhaps engage you." Even if that call doesn't come in, the client is much more likely to reach out to you early about the next opportunity. Many Activators who have lost opportunities but stayed in touch methodically find that later, the work eventually comes. One such Activator, a partner at a large US law firm, put it well: "The best way to build trust is when clients think of you as an advisor that is always around for them, regardless of whether they picked you for that piece of work. There's no better compliment than if they call you for advice on a deal they are working on with someone else. You wouldn't charge for that but that's gold because they are thinking of you when something thorny happens. If I charged you for that advice it's like charging you for the dinner I just took you to."

Summary

The pivot points we've discussed in this chapter are the moments where Activator behaviors, habits, and mindsets come to life. The themes of committing, connecting, and creating help activators turn contacts into new business one activity at a time. By prioritizing time, contacts, and events, Activators make efficient use of their business development time. By using their networks to deliver value and make connections, Activators build a robust network that leads to new opportunities. By consistently delivering insights and value across that network, they turn conversations into opportunity and build long-term relationships. By being other-focused and taking an integrative approach, they avoid subjecting themselves and their clients to lose-lose negotiations. And, finally, by focusing on the need to protect the relationship, they bounce back from client setbacks and lay the groundwork for new business and deeper partnership with their clients.

— 7 —

Building an Activator Firm

One thing we constantly impress on firm leaders is that Activator is a story that is not just about individual skills, but also about firm-level capabilities. For a firm to effectively transform itself into an Activator firm, it needs not just professionals who can demonstrate Activator behaviors, but a platform that supports and enables this approach at the firm level. Every part of the firm must be aligned in support of it—learning and development, content and event marketing, business development, technology, incentives and rewards, culture, and leadership.[1] In very real terms, this means that an Activator transformation at the firm level is not for the faint of heart. It cannot be accomplished by simply reading this book or listening to a keynote or podcast about the research. It requires full commitment, lest it become the latest "flavor of the week"—something leaders talk about in firmwide communications or at the partner retreat but nothing that drives sustained and meaningful change.

In our research, we identified a handful of firms across various segments of professional services that have gotten Activator behaviors to stick—in no small part because they have been willing to align the entire firm to this mission. Their experiences surfaced several key lessons that leaders looking to drive Activator transformations in their own firms should follow.

Hiring and Selecting Activators

Traditionally, firms have focused on technical expertise, client impact, and book of business as the criteria for making partner selection and lateral hiring decisions. But our research suggests that other criteria should be emphasized as well; for instance, a candidate's proclivity for collaboration. This is particularly important for firms that use the hiring of partners from competitor firms as a growth lever. Bringing in Confidants or Experts from other firms—even if they are proven rainmakers—can be a costly mistake if they refuse to collaborate or can't cultivate an Activator mindset.

Hiring Activators (or screening for Activator potential in partner candidates) requires a behavioral interviewing approach that digs more deeply into the *how* of a candidate's business development performance. In conversations with leaders from a variety of firms, we heard a number of effective interview questions that leaders have used to distill a candidate's Activator proclivity. Here are a few examples:

- How much time do you allocate to business development per week?

- Can you describe your personal business development routine? How do you spend your time?

- Who is your ideal client? What do you look for to decide whether a client will be a good fit for you?

- Can you describe your book of business to me? Is it heavily concentrated with a few key clients or spread across a larger number of clients?

- Can you tell me about how you manage your professional network?

- What are your thoughts about platforms like LinkedIn—good, bad, indifferent? If you consider it a useful platform for business development, can you walk me through how you use it?

- Have you ever used LinkedIn or another networking platform to identify an opportunity that led to a new client relationship or helped you deepen an existing client relationship? Can you tell me about that experience?

- How do you spend your time at events and conferences?

- Do you have a system or process that helps you manage your critical contacts?

- Can you tell me about a time you walked a colleague into one of your clients and how that impacted the client relationship?

- Have you ever had to knit together capabilities from across your firm to deliver a solution to a client? Can you tell me about that?

- Can you share a time you proactively brought an idea or opportunity to a client that the client themselves had yet to realize?

- How does what you do for clients tie to their ability to make money, save money, or mitigate risk?

- Can you tell me about a time when you supported a client's personal goals or objectives in a way that the client wasn't expecting?

In addition to these behavioral questions, leaders can look at external markers, especially on platforms like LinkedIn. How big is a candidate's professional network? How often are they posting, commenting on, or liking others' posts? Have they observed these candidates at events like industry conferences? And, if so, how were they spending their time?

For firms with a deficit of Activators, a smart way to deploy this scarce talent (until others can be hired or trained to be Activators) is to assign them to be relationship managers on the firm's largest and highest-potential client opportunities—something that a number of progressive organizations, like law firm Faegre Drinker, strive to do.[2] While the other four professional profiles—Expert, Confidant, Debater, and Realist—have certain strengths and can add to the diversity and impact of a client-facing team, firms would be well-advised to make sure the person running point for their largest clients fits the Activator mold.

Training Activators

McDermott Will & Emery has a unique approach to business development, a key component of which is a global training program for partners on managing their networks. Over the past five years, the firm has trained over five hundred partners, resulting in stronger client relationships and helping to increase firm revenue. The firm has grown from $800 million to $1.8 billion, making it the fastest-growing law firm in the United States.[3]

Clearly, one of the most important roles a firm's leadership team plays is providing a robust Activator training program for its professionals. As of the date of this book's publication, our team at DCMi has trained thousands of partners and associates in firms across all major segments of professional services and can share some guidance based on that experience.

The first thing for leaders to understand is that their professionals, as a group, generally detest business development training. The very thought of it generates eye rolls and excuses as to why they can't attend. In our experience, these reactions are a function both of what's being taught and how it's being taught. Most business development training doesn't resonate with professionals either because it's designed for B2B salespeople or because it's based on anecdotal evidence and personal opinion about how to engage clients and win business. "The biggest challenge we had rolling out Activator at our firm," said the CBDO of a large law firm, "was the fact that we'd burned a lot of trust and goodwill among our partners with the training we'd run them through in the past. The feedback was pretty universal that it wasn't credible or relevant, so we had some rebuilding to do to convince them that it would be different this time around." For these reasons, we typically recommend that firms start small: pilot with a small group, collect feedback, tune the program, and expand from there.

The importance of cohort-based learning

This brings up a related, critical point: the best way to deliver Activator training is through small, carefully constructed cohorts. This is not simply because cohort-based learning tends to be stickier than the traditional ballroom-style "sheep dip" approach to learning (given the greater amount of discussion and interaction that happens in a smaller group), but because it harnesses the active ingredients of the Activator model. Recall that a central pillar of the Activator approach is collaborating with other professionals across the firm. One of the biggest obstacles to collaboration is the fact that professionals from different offices and practice areas simply don't know their colleagues and therefore don't have the confidence to bring them to a longtime client for fear of what might go wrong.

At nearly every partner retreat we attend, firm leaders will implore their colleagues to "sit next to somebody you don't know at lunch" in the hopes that this will jump-start collaboration. But this sort of guidance, however well-intended, won't get professionals who are reluctant to collaborate with colleagues to suddenly do so. Instead, we've found that an intensive, shared experience like participating in a training cohort with a dozen colleagues you've never met before is much more effective at breaking down barriers to collaboration than almost anything else a firm can do. Not surprisingly, one of the biggest benefits we hear from firms who pursue this cohort-based approach is that, following the training, their professionals identify and pursue opportunities to jointly engage specific clients.

The two big drawbacks of cohort-based learning are difficulty scaling the training across large organizations and having to put much more design thought into cohort construction than one would in a ballroom-like setting where all professionals are being trained together. There are some things that firms can do to scale cohort-based learning more quickly—for instance, relying on internal teams to deliver the training—but we believe that the far greater stickiness of cohort-based learning outweighs any scale disadvantages. Nearly every firm has had the expensive and frustrating experience of paying an outside vendor to train a large group of professionals at the partner retreat only to have most of what was taught end up being forgotten and professionals reverting back to what they were doing before. Cohort-based learning is ultimately designed to avoid this outcome.

Cohort design is something that we find firms sometimes overlook, but it is a critical determinant of whether the training delivers its intended benefit. A simple but useful framework comes from one of our senior faculty, Larry Murphy, a former executive at Morgan Stanley and learning and development leader at McKinsey as well as several top business schools:

> In designing and delivering senior-level programming, I think it's helpful to think about a firm's senior professionals as either learners, "tourists," or "prisoners." Learners are eager to pick up new skills and understand the behaviors that will lead to greater success. They're hungry for feedback and development opportunities, including formal training. Tourists are on the fence. They are open to learning experiences but unsure if they'll see the benefit themselves. This skepticism tends to be rooted in bad experiences they've had in previous training. Perhaps they felt it was a waste of their time—their most precious and constrained resource—and didn't help them to improve in the ways they expected. And prisoners are just that—prisoners in the room, because they'd rather be somewhere else. They're imprisoned by being stuck in their ways and not open to learning new approaches. Some may be high performers who feel like they've figured it out already, whereas others may be average

performers but figure they're only a few years shy of retirement, and things are going OK, so "Why change things up now?"

Obviously, firms will want to identify and target learners for new training experiences like an Activator cohort. Who are the ideal learners for a training cohort? In our experience, they generally fall into three categories: newly promoted partners, lateral hires, and tenured professionals who are looking for a "reset" moment. In most firms we work with, professionals do not get much business development experience before they make partner. But when they do earn that long-awaited promotion, it comes with a new expectation: that they generate client work, not just deliver it. This can be a scary moment for new partners who've spent the preceding six to eight years honing their craft as lawyers, accountants, consultants, and the like, only to be thrown into the deep end of the pool and asked to do something they've never been trained to do. We often recommend to firms heading down an Activator path that this is the population they should target first. Lateral hires from outside of private practice—for instance, government lawyers hired in as law firm partners or experienced corporate communications leaders brought in as PR agency partners—are also an excellent population to target. Like new partners, they are deep subject matter experts but almost entirely lacking in business development skills.

Aside from these obvious groups, how do firms identify other eager learners from across their partnerships and avoid degrading the cohort experience by mistakenly inviting prisoners to participate? We've seen two approaches be particularly effective. The first involves running a pilot cohort and then presenting the Activator story at the partner retreat followed by a panel of pilot cohort participants who share their experiences having gone through the training. After the panel, the firm distributes a survey asking its professionals to express their interest (or lack thereof) in being a part of an upcoming cohort. This is a surefire way to identify eager learners. The second approach involves deploying a pre-cohort survey designed to assess each participant's sense of their own personal effectiveness across a range of Activator skills and behaviors as well as their openness to learning how to improve on each dimension. Invariably, tourists will yield mixed results. Prisoners will yield results that are skewed toward already believing they are very effective and/or not being open to behavior change.

While enthusiastic learners are clearly in the wheelhouse for new training programs, firms shouldn't ignore the tourists or the prisoners. In our experience, tourists will come along once they hear the positive feedback from colleagues; firms just need to create the "pull-through" demand that gets them to ask for a seat in a cohort versus being told they must attend. Prisoners, on the other hand, need to be managed carefully. When firms force prisoners to attend business development training, the best outcome is that they waste their professionals' time and the firm's money. A far worse outcome is that they willfully disrupt the cohort, thereby poisoning the well for other participants. At the same time, *excluding* these professionals—especially those who are seen as top performers by their colleagues—can be a noticeable omission that can damage the brand of the program internally. The best approach to managing these strong personalities is to pull them aside and enlist their support in the training by asking them to reinforce the teaching by sharing their own experiences. "We've managed to harness some of these partners by asking them to serve as role models for the newer partners in the cohort given the success they've had in their careers," one law firm CMO explained to us. "Asking them to serve in this capacity typically leads to them being enthusiastic advocates for what's being taught by the instructor. Ironically, in the end, most of them end up leaving the cohorts saying 'Wow, I learned a lot more than I thought I would!'"

One final word about the best populations to target with Activator training. Where most firms will wait until professionals make partner to give them business development training, the best firms do this much earlier in a professional's career, introducing the core tenets of being an Activator years earlier when professionals are at the associate or manager level. Activator behaviors—like creating a business development routine or purposefully building one's professional network—are things that can and should be taught much earlier in a professional's career.

More to the point, firms are struggling to retain their most talented associates, a huge percentage of whom end up leaving for other pursuits because they don't like life in a professional services firm. The CEO of one of the world's largest law firms laid out the challenge plainly: "We make a big investment in our early-career professionals. Like other firms, a disappointingly low percentage of them end up sticking around for the next six to seven years to make partner. Investing in training them to be more effective business developers early in their careers is a no-brainer. It shows we're committed to helping them make this critical leap so they can contribute to the firm's growth."

Reskilling internal teams as Activator coaches

Most professional services organizations have internal business development—staff functions that exist to help partners target and win client opportunities. The members of these teams are not practitioners like the bulk of the firm's people (i.e., they are typically not lawyers, accountants, etc.) but instead have deep expertise in the selling and marketing of professional services.

Because business development is not a partner's full-time job, the business development team is a critical function that keeps the wheels of business development turning across the firm—even when partners are busy delivering client work. Unfortunately, at most professional services firms, these teams are viewed and treated as back-office or sales admin support by busy partners. Typically, this means updating CRM records, filling out RFPs, preparing pitch materials, and cataloging partner, practice, and sector-level credentials to be showcased in client meetings. And the team's performance is commonly based on whether the partner was happy with the team's support, not whether business was won or lost. Leading firms, however, are rethinking this model and positioning their business development teams to deliver greater value to partners than what they've been permissioned to deliver historically.

In 2021, Eversheds Sutherland's firm leaders were on a mission to create a successful path for those on the partnership track. It became apparent during the Covid-19 pandemic that the business development skills needed to succeed were limited and the ability to engage in business development via traditional avenues, including events and visits to client offices, were nonexistent. "It was evident that our BD team should be doing more to prepare our senior associates before they are even considered for partner," explains Erin Meszaros, the firm's global chief client officer.

To address this challenge, Meszaros did two unconventional things. First, she deployed a senior associate business development training program focused on teaching early-career professionals Activator skills, something that most firms don't do until professionals reach the partner level. Second, she tasked her business development team with teaching the course. "Not only does the program help instill the fundamentals of being an Activator at an early point in their careers—which improves their odds of making partner and becoming successful client developers—but because the BD team leads the training, it helps build a stronger relationship between these professionals and the internal BD team. This combination avoids the stigma that business development is low-value work and increases the opportunity for success," Meszaros explains.

The firm is intentional about the way cohorts are designed. Participants are hand-picked to allow associates around the world to come together in a collaborative, cross-firm environment that they haven't experienced. Between weekly course modules, participants are asked to apply the Activator skills they learn with clients and report back on what worked and what didn't. Established Activators from across the firm's senior partner ranks sit in on these report-back sessions to provide their own feedback, perspective, and encouragement to the cohort participants.

The work the Eversheds team does to build greater internal connection with associates through their training programs has contributed to impressive results. In terms of revenue, 2023 was the most successful year in the history of the firm. And the firm's next generation of partners is arriving better equipped to build successful business development skills: eight out of the last ten people most recently promoted to partner had completed the firm's Activator business development training as senior associates.

Avoiding common sales training traps

As we've mentioned, one of the biggest gripes professionals have about business development training is that they see it as sales training. There are several reasons for this. First, as we've noted previously, sales is a process, whereas client development in professional services is a cycle. Sales professionals take leads (typically furnished by marketing), qualify those opportunities, sell to them, and close them—after which, they hand the new clients over to the teams responsible for delivering the product or solution. Professionals, on the other hand, target and engage opportunities (that they have typically surfaced from their own networks), sell to them, and close them but are then also responsible for delivering the work and renewing and expanding the client relationship (which often involves hunting for new opportunities within existing client accounts). Any business development training for professionals that doesn't acknowledge this critical distinction—and doesn't reflect these important role differences in terms of the skills required to be successful—is over before it begins. Our strong advice to any firm leader, irrespective of whether they choose an Activator approach or something else, is to not waste their time or their firm's money on traditional B2B sales training for this very important reason.

A second shortcoming of B2B sales training is that it tends to be more focused on skill development than behavior change. With very few exceptions, most sales training programs begin from the assumption that somebody who is in sales already has the right mindset, behaviors, and motivation to sell. What they need is to harness these raw capabilities and apply them more productively in the market. What they don't need is to be convinced to sell. Training professionals is the opposite. Business development training in professional services starts with the assumption that most learners didn't get into their chosen professions because they wanted to sell; they pursued those professions because they wanted to be lawyers, accountants, consultants, engineers, and so on. Therefore, there should be much more time spent developing the right mindsets and behaviors that can support effective business development.

How does this translate in terms of curriculum? Most B2B sales training tends to be very focused on how to follow specific processes and use specific tools to make sales reps more effective. A professional services business development curriculum, because it's more rooted in behavior change than process or tool adoption, will delve as deeply into the social science research underpinning client buying behavior as well as the habits, mindsets, and behaviors of top-performing professionals. In practical terms, this makes a professional services program feel less like a training class and more like a graduate seminar.

One final difference is that most sales training is designed to show salespeople *what to do.* This is because, once a sales methodology is chosen by a company's sales leaders, the only option for sales reps is compliance. Those who choose not to follow the prescribed approach are shown the door. In most professional services firms, however, the partners are the owners—which means that they can choose to follow the training they're provided or not. So a professional services program will be more about providing general guidance than specific step-by-step instructions. It's as much about *how to think* than about what, specifically, to do in any given client situation, in other words.

Enabling Activators

Becoming an Activator requires sustained focus if the lessons are to stick beyond the initial training. Fortunately, firm leaders have a number of levers at their disposal to send signals to their professionals indicating preferred activities or to create conditions that nudge them in certain directions. In our research, we identified several leading firms that have, through their unique approaches to BD team support, marketing, or technology enablement, effectively made an Activator approach to business development feel both obvious and easy to professionals.

Using events as a platform for activation

One of the standout examples of using firm resources to encourage Activator behaviors is how law firm McDermott Will & Emery approaches its firm-sponsored events.

When Ira Coleman ascended to the chairmanship of McDermott, one of his top priorities was to establish a firmwide commitment to business development. He felt that many partners missed a crucial fact about this core part of their jobs: "Most partners will say they got into this profession because they want to help people. They don't realize that business development *is* about helping people—connecting with them, understanding what they need, and offering a solution." Still, Coleman found that no amount of public or private urging would get those partners who were reluctant to engage in business development to do so. Instead, the firm needed to make Activator-like business development the path of least resistance for their partners.

One of the biggest opportunities to do this, Coleman's team decided, was to manage their firm-sponsored events differently. After all, these are controlled environments run by the firm, which meant they could exert a disproportionate influence on how their lawyers spent their time and interacted with clients. Because these are "home field" settings, they also represented a safe space for reluctant business developers to perform Activator-like client engagement. "Events," Coleman explains, "give us the best chance to turn our reluctant Experts into Activators."

At Coleman's direction, the firm's business development and marketing team built a standard playbook for all firm-sponsored events that consists of three primary components: goal-setting, targeting, and engineering.

Goal-setting. Many firms run their own events but few, if any, measure the ROI of their events. At best, they look at attendee satisfaction scores to gauge whether the event was a success. McDermott actually sets business development impact targets for each event and uses these to assess whether an event is worth investing in. The firm's leaders expect to see positive ROI from any event within six months—whether the event is big, small, formal, or informal. The clarity of this goal helps team members make better decisions about where to invest their time, efforts, and resources. "One of our goals is to ensure that we are growing our work with the people we've connected with at events—either opening new matters with new or existing clients or, at a minimum, deepening client engagement in a way that will lead to future work," explains the firm's chief business development and marketing officer, Elizabeth Gooch.

What should the ROI of an event be? Our team at DCMi has found this to vary a bit across different segments, but our research suggests that a 5× return is at once aspirational enough to be stretchy for most firms but not so high that it is unattainable without flawless execution. Put simply, this means that a successful event will return five times the cost of the event in new client business. The 5× target should also influence the decisions made about which events to continue hosting, attending, or sponsoring, based on their historical performance.

Targeting. Most lawyers attend events and hope that they make some connections or engage in conversations that lead to client work. McDermott is far more intentional and works to make sure these encounters are not left to chance. For any firm-sponsored event, the team targets contacts to be invited or engaged during the event. The business development team uses client feedback survey responses, post-matter interview notes and account-level engagement data, recent thought leadership downloads, and recent billings trendlines to curate an invitation list for any event.

Aside from helping to build a curated invitation list, McDermott uses this targeting exercise to identify partners to serve as speakers and panelists at their events—in other words, to identify who they want to put in front of a specific audience. "We make heavy use of our partners as moderators at our events," explains Gooch. "This helps us to showcase specific capabilities depending on the audience." Coleman adds that these opportunities help partners who major in the Expert profile act like Activators: "We see this all the time with our best Experts. We put them on panels, and they have a chance to demonstrate their knowledge and skill. Then they go to the VIP dinner afterward, and people are coming up to them to network and, suddenly, they're acting like Activators without prompting."

Engineering. In the leadup to any event, McDermott's business development team makes sure firm participants are prepared for the conversations they want to have at the event. For firm-hosted events, their lawyers are required to submit a simple business plan in order to earn an invitation. They are asked to identify the clients and prospective clients they plan to engage, brainstorm conversations they hope to have, and even list out questions they plan to ask if they have the opportunity. Without submitting a detailed plan in advance, a lawyer isn't allowed to attend a firm-sponsored event, and if it is a third-party event, expense reimbursement is approved only after a lawyer has shared the conversations they had and connections they made at the event.

McDermott doesn't leave the success of an event to chance. For any non-McDermott client attending the event, the business development team conducts pre-event calls to learn more about what the client hopes to gain from attending. The team will also conduct pre-calls with their lawyers to game-plan and assist them in setting up coffees, lunches, and other one-on-one meetings in advance. "We're trying to make it straightforward for them. It doesn't need to feel overwhelming. Guidance and preparation help lawyers create pathways that move the needle," explains Gooch.

After any event, the marketing or business development team plays a critical role in hosting timely debriefs with firm participants to capture insights, takeaways, or client commitments. Lawyers are expected to diligently follow up with contacts in the days immediately following the event—and failure to do so could negatively impact their ability to attend future events.

. . .

Perhaps no other event captures the success of McDermott's events playbook better than their signature health care event, HPE Miami, which has grown from a 40-person event fifteen years ago to an industry destination with more than 1,500 annual attendees. The planning and intention pay off, with the firm's lawyers understanding how to activate potential before, during, and after any event. And the results are clear in McDermott's fantastic multiyear growth rate. "The way we manage and run events has become one of our superpowers as a firm," says McDermott's Coleman.

Reinforcing Activator behaviors with technology

The professional services industry is littered with stories of firms that have wasted millions on technology purchases in the hope that, by providing the right tools, their reluctant and ineffective business developers will suddenly be transformed into rainmakers. In many respects, software vendors are to blame for selling the same promise to professional services firms that they sell B2B sales teams—when the two types of organizations couldn't be more different.

For example, few, if any, firms can mandate that their professionals use a specific piece of technology. And in many firms, professionals operate under the view that their clients are just that: *their* clients, not the firm's clients, so they question any attempt by their firms to capture information about their client relationships and interactions. Fee-earners are busy; learning software that is often not built for the segment and is difficult to use is not high on their to-do lists.

This is not to say, of course, that technology isn't a central part of the Activator story. Quite the contrary. Our research clearly shows that Activators are heavy users of relationship intelligence platforms, knowledge management tools, and CRM. Such technology helps them build, track, and manage their professional networks, collaborate with colleagues across their organizations, and stay on top of business development activities that need to be done, among other things. In fact, in many of our interviews, Activators spoke openly about the fact that they either had to cobble together their own solutions—for example, managing their networks and client development activities using spreadsheets—or that they bought their own licenses to technologies they felt would help them in the market.

The key point for firm leaders to remember is that, in a professional services setting, technology can reinforce existing behaviors, but it can't by itself conjure new behaviors. If professionals don't understand the importance of Activator behaviors or if they understand their importance but lack the skills to effectively apply them, no amount of technology spend can overcome this. But if professionals are equipped with the right training and coaching on how to engage clients like Activators, if internal obstacles are removed and culture and incentives are all aligned to support an Activator approach, technology can be the glue that makes Activator behaviors stick and come to life.

Laura Saklad, vice president of Legal Industry at Intapp, explains that "Supporting the business development efforts of busy professionals with technology really comes down to three things: personalizing the user experience so that it's relevant and efficient for the individual; surfacing timely insights and recommendations about clients, relationships, and opportunities at pivotal moments; and providing the tools to quickly take action on those recommendations. When you deliver those benefits to professionals, it's not hard to get them to use the technology." It's not unlike the fitness trackers we wear around our wrists. If one fails to appreciate the importance of living an active lifestyle or doesn't understand the behavior change required to get fit, well, then it's just an expensive bracelet.

CRM as an Activator platform. Global law firm Bird & Bird integrates technology into its business development training and coaching program. The program, which is delivered by the firm's business development team, includes customized elements designed to show partners how to use their CRM platform, Intapp's DealCloud, to engage in Activator business development activities. Team members also fan out for in-office trainings where features are demonstrated with emphasis on how other Activators successfully use the system. "We can't force partners to use every feature," says Sophie Bowkett, Bird & Bird's CMO, "but we can spread stories around our offices about how and why our best Activators are using the CRM tool. After seeing it live, people are often more willing to share their contact and activity details in the system."

Finnegan, a leading intellectual property law firm, uses a CRM that includes features allowing partners to schedule follow-up tasks after meetings and receive reminders to reach out after certain time intervals. These capabilities simultaneously save their partners time while also ensuring that data is up-to-date and reliable. They also leverage their firmwide experience management platform to capture deep insights into practices, industries, courts, judges, clients, court filings, and the varied technical experience of the firm's intellectual property (IP) professionals. Using that catalog of the firm's collective work experience, technical expertise, and subject-matter profiles, partners can easily identify and spotlight the colleagues who bring the right skills, knowledge, and expertise to potential engagements, and thereby win more work from existing and new clients.

Leveraging technology to help professionals connect broadly and deeply. Technology also plays a critical role in helping professionals build, manage, and leverage their networks—a cornerstone of the Activator approach. Capstone Partners, one of the largest middle-market investment banking firms in the United States, uses relationship intelligence software to reveal connections between its partners and prospects. That firm uses the technology to apply relationship scores to colleagues, contacts, and clients, and then builds highly targeted buyer lists based on that data. This helps ensure effective outreach and streamlined communication between partners, clients, and prospects. The technology also helps bankers to quickly identify the right person to contact at each target company and to capture and track touchpoints and interactions with prospects, making lead-generation efforts more efficient.[4]

Morrinson Wealth, a financial services firm based in London, uses LinkedIn Sales Navigator to help their advisors find prospective clients and build better sales pipelines. The firm's business development team trains advisors to use LinkedIn, helping them to build and target ideal client profiles and personalize their outreach and engagement efforts. The business development team guides advisers on how to post content to attract clients they haven't spoken to yet, like or comment on potential client posts (especially to demonstrate that an advisor understands a client's needs and interests early in the relationship), and distribute content through the messaging channel to help nudge clients who might be on the fence, among other activities. The investment to equip the team has paid off handsomely, with a 33.8 percent increase in new business leads compared with the year before the platform was deployed. And, when compared with other lead-generation sources Morrinson relies on, LinkedIn has ranked highest in conversion to client.

The promise of AI. As of the date of this book's publication, most platforms used by professionals will include AI-powered capabilities. No technology holds greater potential for helping professionals improve their business development effectiveness. From expediting simple tasks like writing emails to helping professionals with more complex activities such as identifying incremental growth opportunities within accounts, AI holds the promise of finally answering the "What's in it for me?" question for professionals when it comes to using the technology their firms have invested in.

Software providers are quickly working to bring the promise of AI into their platforms—turning technologies like CRM from tools professionals *have* to use into tools they *want* to use by building in nudges and other in-the-moment coaching that can help professionals become better business developers. Intapp, for instance, has built an entire Activator solution into its CRM that is designed to prompt professionals on Activator behaviors and activities. For example, the system provides a personalized feed for professionals that guides and supports their business development time. It alerts them to key executive role changes based on data feeds from third-party relationship intelligence providers and indicates the relationship health of current clients based on data in email, calendar, time-tracking, and billing systems. And using AI, it suggests insights to use when engaging clients and prospective clients based on recent market events, regulatory changes, and the firm's history with the client's organization—even providing the first draft of an email to use when reaching out to a client.

Global law firm Taylor Wessing uses software to automatically capture contact data from email communications to enrich client records and identify cross-selling opportunities—all without their lawyers having to manually input data into the system. This "zero-entry" data capture also helps keep client records fresh and up to date, avoiding the problems that arise if lawyers are not regularly updating such information. With this data in hand, Taylor Wessing has also created a series of dashboards that are user-driven, specific to the partner and their client accounts. A client dashboard, for instance, shows a system-generated relationship score based on recent levels of communications and meetings, financial and billing information, and a projection based on historical data that gives the partner a sense for areas where fees are lower than expected for a particular practice group.

The business development and marketing team at Taylor Wessing work to remind the partners of the value of having such data and the necessity of using it. "Taylor Wessing has a very client-driven culture, and our people really value tools that enable them to proactively engage with clients. Data-driven decision-making is part of our DNA, and these tools really create a competitive advantage for us," explains Holly Adams, head of MarTech and Operations at Taylor Wessing. "The tool doesn't read your email. It just knows the email was sent or received and tracks nothing about what happens inside of that exchange. We needed to be very clear that it links back to our strategy, to keeping clients close, and to winning more work. And we are continually reminding them."

Intapp CEO John Hall sees a brave new world for technology and how it will be used by professionals in the advisory, legal, and capital markets verticals the company serves. He explains:

> Intelligence is our clients' competitive advantage. They deliver value by leveraging their expertise, relationships, and experience. To enable an Activator mindset, firms should focus both on in-

stilling new behaviors and on implementing AI-enabled software that reinforces these client interaction and relationship best practices. Fundamentally, we believe the possibility enabled by AI will have an outsized impact on these professionals and markets by accelerating both the work they do and how they build relationships. The firms and professionals who best apply AI to activating their firms' intelligence and relationships will be the big winners.

David Chun, CEO of Equilar, sees AI as the breakthrough that professionals have been waiting for:

> A big part of being an Activator is about staying on top of the changes in one's network so that you can spot changes in the market and act on them with speed and precision. Unfortunately, for most professionals, this has been an incredibly manual task. They've had to sort through a whole range of data sources and hope that they spotted movement in the market before their competitors. It's impossible for the average professional to stay on top of it all—especially when they are simultaneously executing client work. AI promises to change all of this by pulling together disparate data sources and feeding real-time data and alerts to professionals so that they never miss an opportunity.

Aligning client teams to the Activator model

One of the best places for a firm to realize the benefits of an Activator approach to client engagement is in its key client program. Key clients are those accounts that offer an opportunity for a firm to bring the breadth of its capabilities to bear—to expand beyond single-line-of-service work and engage clients on their most complex and demanding needs. Doing this requires professionals from different practice areas and offices to team up and collaborate, something that comes naturally to Activators.

Leading firms like Baker McKenzie are deliberate in making investments in their client programs to drive firmwide collaboration. Baker McKenzie invests in clients in which the firm has the deepest relationships and where there is the most opportunity—typically because of their demonstrated receptivity to differentiators like cross-border support and sector knowledge. "We know the practices that are beachheads for us, where follow-on sustainable growth is far more likely," explains Angela Petros, the firm's global CMO. Accounts are then tiered, with different tiers receiving differing value-adds and levels of extra support tailored to a client's needs. Client team leaders are designated by the firm's leadership team with input from Petros's marketing leadership team. And the client teams are designed specifically to include partners with demonstrated Activator tendencies to maximize the potential for collaboration and cross-selling the firm's capabilities. The firm also invests in training its attorneys on Activator behaviors to improve the level of service delivered to clients. The teams meet regularly to strategize, review client feedback to proactively address any issues or follow up on opportunities, and allocate marketing resources.

Client teams use a series of measures to understand the progress they are making toward their growth goals. On the input side, the number of connections between Baker McKenzie's lawyers and decision-makers and influencers within client accounts is monitored and benchmarked relative to competitors using a variety of technology tools. On the output side, important measures include client revenue, profitability, share of wallet, and number of practices and markets served.

The result is a program that attorneys want to be a part of, due to the increased resourcing and growth potential, and it feels exclusive for clients. "These are investments we're making with intention," explains Petros, "Internally, these are highly sought-after portfolios. Helping to lead a client team means being able to tap into significant firm resources to grow accounts in a collaborative way."

Incentivizing and Rewarding Activator Behaviors

Perhaps no topic causes more angst in professional services firms than the subject of compensation and rewards. For most firms, it's a "third rail" topic—strictly to be avoided lest leaders get an earful from disgruntled professionals.

Right up front, it's important to make one thing clear: *firms cannot turn their professionals into Activators by paying them to do so.* If professionals would not otherwise behave in an Activator way—committing to business development, connecting and collaborating, and proactively creating value for clients—no amount of pay will get them to suddenly change their behaviors.

In fact, most research suggests that pay is not a particularly effective tool to get knowledge workers like professionals to do anything. For years, psychologists have studied the differential impact of intrinsic motivators—where motivation comes from within and is driven by internal factors like enjoyment, curiosity, or a sense of fulfillment—and extrinsic motivators—where motivation arises from external factors such as rewards, punishments, or recognition from others. In the mid-1980s, psychologists Edward Deci and Richard Ryan published a book titled *Intrinsic Motivation and Self-Determination in Human Behavior*—research that was more recently explored and popularized by Dan Pink in his book *Drive*.[5] Pink points to numerous studies that conclude that compensation results in better performance within the workplace only if tasks consist of basic mechanical skills. If the task involves cognitive skills, decision-making, creativity, or higher-order thinking—as does all of the work of a fee-earner in professional services—extrinsic motivators actually results in lower performance.

Dr. Larry Richard, who has studied this phenomenon in professional services like law for years, suggests that understanding the power of intrinsic rewards is a key for firm leaders to get their professionals to accept change initiatives. "Deci and Ryan showed that what motivates us are intrinsic rewards like autonomy, belonging, and competence," he maintains:

We want autonomy in the sense that we make meaningful choices that affect our futures. We want to belong to something bigger than ourselves. And because it means something to us, we want to master it and get good at it. Meaning and purpose runs through all of them. If firms want their people to endlessly perform, they will tap into motivators like doing things that matter to them—making a difference in the world, feeling like they control their destiny, feeling like they are connected to people in a meaningful way, feeling like they've mastered some competency. Those are intrinsic rewards that have all been empirically tested and will produce endless amounts of motivation. Don't get hung up on dangling shiny extrinsic rewards like bonuses and luxury goods.

None of this is to say, however, that aligning compensation to Activator behaviors isn't important. On the contrary, it's crucially important—but not for the reasons most leaders think. Rewarding Activator behaviors is important not to *get* professionals to behave like Activators but to recognize that they already *are*. Aligning compensation to Activator behaviors helps to close the "say-do" gap that arises when professionals are told to do one thing but then paid to do something very different—a problem that can undermine the firm's broader Activator transformation efforts, no matter how well designed, resourced, and executed those efforts are.

On countless occasions, we have met professionals who roll their eyes when their leaders exhort them to "play as a team" and to "bring the whole of the firm to our clients." At a recent partner retreat, one accountant told us, "Talk is cheap. We've been beating this drum of collaboration for years now but continue to shower the most comp on sharp-elbowed Confidants who wouldn't be caught dead walking a colleague into one of their client accounts. We all know it's toxic and runs exactly counter to what we're trying to accomplish, but our leaders are too scared of losing their top rainmakers to change the compensation system in a way that aligns with what they're preaching."

Fortunately, our research surfaced some compelling examples of firms willing to break the traditional professional services compensation model and align their pay and rewards with the behaviors they are trying to encourage across their partnerships.

Rewarding collaboration

Around 2016, Russell Reynolds Associates (RRA), a global talent advisory and executive search firm, had identified two priority areas for improvement: collaboration and apprenticeship. While RRA's leaders felt they'd made good progress on both fronts, they recognized that their consultants' compensation wasn't aligned to the new direction of the firm.

Historically, RRA consultants were compensated based on three key measures:

- *Lead generation.* For every dollar of revenue from a client, the consultant who first received the call from that client would be credited with a dollar of lead generation fees.

- *Expertise fees.* For every dollar of revenue from a client, the consultant who earned the lead generation for an engagement could reward other consultants who helped win the work with up to a dollar of expertise fees (without reducing the credit from the lead generation the originating consultant received).

- *Execution fees.* For every dollar of revenue from a client, the consultant who executed the engagement would be credited with a dollar of execution fees.[6]

The firm had long used a discretionary, nonformulaic compensation system where quartiles and rank at the end of a year had a large impact on bonus—with exponential bonus payouts possible for top-ranked individuals. While firm priorities like collaboration and apprenticeship were considered when determining rankings, most consultants felt that the system was heavily tilted toward lead generation, sending mixed signals about how important these priorities really were to the firm.

James Roome, head of RRA's London office at the time, explains that the lead-generation-focused measurement approach was "rotting away the culture of collaboration that we were aiming to create."[7] According to Bruno Bolzan, then the firm's CHRO, "The next generation of consultants felt they weren't getting a chance to showcase what they could do because they weren't invited to any pitches for client work. We needed them to learn and grow, but they were at the mercy of the top people in the firm who didn't want to relinquish opportunities."[8]

To bridge this disconnect, the firm decided to change the measures used to determine compensation, combining lead generation and expertise into a single measure that they called "Winning Business." This new measure would equal up to 200 percent of revenues for a given project. The originating consultant could earn a maximum of 100 percent of the project amount but they could allocate an additional 100 percent to recognize any colleagues who helped win the business. As Clarke Murphy, then CEO, explained, "Apprenticeship and collaboration are the long-term growth of the firm. We showed that we will pay more when our consultants work together and when they teach others to do high-quality work."[9]

Like any change that impacts compensation, there were some teething problems with the rollout of the new measurement system. Namely, RRA had to work through the challenge of certain consultants gaming the system—for instance, giving extra credit to colleagues in exchange for them shouldering more of the execution burden or creating "IOU" situations in which one consultant would be overly generous in providing credit in order to solicit future reciprocity from colleagues. "Some more aggressive consultants won't take on a project to execute unless they know there is some Winning Business credit in it for them," current CEO Constantine Alexandrakis said in 2021, "which to me feels contrary to our core values."[10] RRA leaders report that these gaming situations have since receded into the background.

An additional concern was top rainmakers leaving the firm because the new model rewarded them less handsomely than the old model. But RRA executives report that they saw far fewer consultant defections than they anticipated.

A key reason for this, they explain, is that the new model encourages generosity—something that is central to the firm's values and a powerful intrinsic motivator for consultants who have chosen to pursue careers with RRA. "The program encourages a sense of growth, optimism, and bringing other people along," says Bolzan.[11] With the underlying measures tied to compensation now aligned to the firm's priorities, RRA has seen collaboration and apprenticeship scores in its annual consultant survey go up every year from 2016 to 2021. In those five years, the firm nearly doubled in size. As Alexandrakis explains, "There has been a dramatic boost to being a collaborative culture. There is more teaming and connectivity and co-ownership of client relationships. By reducing the importance of who gets the call, we've aligned the way we reward our consultants with our emphasis on inclusive teaming."[12]

Moving to fully team-based incentives

Management consulting firm Guidehouse is another powerful example of an organization that has overhauled its compensation model to reward Activator behaviors.

Guidehouse was formed in 2018 when PwC spun off its government consulting unit. PwC alumnus and new Guidehouse CEO Scott McIntyre and his leadership team immediately faced a daunting task: How to differentiate the newly launched business and compete with often far bigger and more established competitors, some of which had been in the industry for over a hundred years? "Our team had a reputation for delivering quality work," he explained, "but, for the first time, we couldn't rely on the PwC brand to help us in the market."

To guide this effort, McIntyre gathered his leadership team and asked them a simple question: "What is it that clients hate about working with consultants?" The team quickly identified a number of dissatisfiers they'd learned from their collective experience. One of the biggest? Clients think they're hiring a firm when they engage a consultancy, but more often than not, they are actually getting support from available, if talented, individuals. So when clients need to leverage the real global breadth of a firm's capabilities, it's often on them to knit together the solution they need. Many consulting leaders and professionals aren't organized or incentivized to do it for them. "As we compared ourselves to our larger competitors, who had the distinct advantage of scale over our then-startup firm, it struck us: our teamwork can beat their scale," McIntyre recalled, "If we can always and reliably work seamlessly together, our team—consisting of 1,200 consultants at the time—could deliver more value to clients than many of our competitors' 100,000 consultants working independently."

Guidehouse feared that a traditional consulting firm model would be an obstacle to teaming, particularly when it came to business development efforts. Too many pitches in consulting firms, McIntyre explained, are handled by the person who happens to get the call, not the team that is objectively best positioned to support the client: "The credibility half-life starts to get pretty steep when the pitch material contains an impressive library of capabilities and slick artifacts but it becomes clear during the pitch that the person delivering it has little personal experience on the opportunity the client is looking to address."

That being said, asking partners to proactively collaborate on new business opportunities and getting them to actually do it are often two different things, especially in firms that have long built their go-to-market approaches around individual expertise and incentives.

As part of Guidehouse's transformation from a collection of individual consultants to a true team-based consultancy providing advisory, digital, and managed services to the public and commercial sectors, their leadership team made the significant decision to eliminate the individual component to their compensation plans. Guidehouse leaders and partners are able to earn a bonus of up to 35 percent of their base salary (or significantly more, if targets are exceeded), with the bonus pool determined entirely by corporate EBITDA (60 percent) and practice-level EBITDA (40 percent). This change—paying exclusively on firm-level and practice-level performance—is part of what McIntyre calls the firm's "no-star model." But it didn't come without its challenges.

Early on in the transition, the firm lost a few rainmakers who did not feel they fit into this culture. That was a cost worth bearing, in McIntyre's view, to provide fluidity to the model and encourage teaming up and down the firm: "We're asking for demonstrated teaming, from our most junior consultants to our most senior partners. We were trying to shift that mindset with rewards and with culture. Other firms might have 10 percent to 20 percent of bonus based on teamwork. Ours is based entirely on that. You'll miss out if you don't collaborate."

When Guidehouse moved to this model, there was some initial heartburn on the leadership team about unanticipated negative effects. After all, many of their best performers were rightly proud of their individual accomplishments. Would eliminating the individual component of incentive compensation reduce motivation? Would some members of the team get too comfortable and create a free rider problem—namely, coasting to a strong bonus on the backs of others? The Guidehouse team set out to hedge these risks in a few ways. First, the bonus program was structured without any caps so that teams are paid for overperformance. Second, leaders at Guidehouse are very comfortable moving the best-fit person to the highest area of opportunity, whether for a new pitch or new market opportunity, while keeping an eye on current client commitments. Finally, Guidehouse consultants' internal reputations are based not just on their personal competence and expertise but on how well they respond to calls from their colleagues to collaborate. Those who are seen to be poor team players are provided coaching and, where necessary, managed out of the organization.

Having signaled the value of teaming in such a transparent way, Guidehouse makes no apologies for acting and moving people out of the system who don't adopt the model. "Failing and not winning is one thing," says McIntyre,

> What's unacceptable is not aggressively teaming to win business and deliver client value. We can't lose that determination to win and deliver as a team. The market is too competitive to tolerate lone wolves and free riders. By getting rid of individual rewards at the director and partner levels, we've eliminated all the questions around who gets credit, how this affects my bonus, etc.

We've eliminated this kind of thinking from our firm, and as a result, our people have become fearless. They can do what's in the best interests of the client and the firm and put aside any concerns that they might get shortchanged in the end.

Guidehouse has successfully built a firm culture around collaboration—a central component of the Activator model—solving for something many firms talk about but few have declared victory on. Its model ensures that the right resources are always put on spotting and winning new client opportunities (as opposed to rewarding the consultant who received the call). "Ninety-nine percent of our partners would point to our collaborative approach to delivering quality work and client value as our core differentiators in the market," says McIntyre. Consultants at all levels take pride in the fact that their clients are comfortable coming to them with questions that may be well beyond their areas of expertise, knowing that their Guidehouse consultant has every incentive to put them in touch with the right consultant or team within the firm rather than hoarding the relationship themselves. To illustrate, Guidehouse recently deployed our Activator diagnostic across their partners and received the highest average score of any firm that has completed it to date—47 percent higher than that of peer organizations.

All of this has led to massive growth for the business. When Guidehouse spun off from PwC, it was a largely Washington, DC–based business, almost entirely focused on the US federal government with a smaller presence in state, local, and municipal governments. All told, the firm was under $600 million in revenue. Today, roughly five and a half years later, the firm employs more than seventeen thousand people in a dozen countries and garners more than $3 billion in revenue. And as a sign that investors are rewarding their unique approach, Guidehouse was recently sold to Bain Capital for $5.3 billion.

Nonmonetary rewards and recognition

Monetary compensation isn't the only part of a firm's rewards system that leaders should align to Activator behaviors. Moments of celebration and recognition send messages to professionals about what the firm values most. As with monetary incentives, we recommend that leaders pass nonmonetary rewards and recognition—whether an official reward like being named an office or practice group leader or an unofficial moment of recognition like a shout-out at a firmwide meeting—through an Activator filter. What about this professional's performance or conduct reinforces Activator mindsets, behaviors, or habits? By the same token, leaders should ask themselves whether a professional they are preparing to recognize publicly has performed in a decidedly non-Activator way— for instance, by hoarding client relationships or by simply burnishing their own credentials in the market and waiting for the phone to ring. Publicly recognizing professionals that the majority of the firm sees as non-Activators can have a particularly outsized impact on early-career professionals who are still trying to figure out what it means to be an effective business developer.

In our research, we surfaced several examples of firms deftly using nonmonetary recognition and rewards to reinforce Activator behaviors. McDermott, for instance, encourages healthy competition among its partners by asking them to log at least two business development activities a week in the firm's CRM system. Qualifying activities must be substantive, such as attending a pitch meeting, networking with contacts at an event, or nonbillable sharing of insights or trends with clients. Firm leaders recognize professionals who demonstrate a steady commitment to developing business, and clients acknowledge the positive impact on their working relationships and support to their businesses.[13]

Baker McKenzie uses its annual self-evaluation memo to signal to its partners the Activator behaviors that matter most to the firm. At most firms, year-end self-appraisals consist of fee-earners' perspectives on their own performance, but Baker McKenzie asks its partners not just to report on their own accomplishments but also point to specific instances in which they've successfully collaborated with colleagues; for example, by introducing other partners with different areas of expertise to their clients. The firm expects its partners to expose clients to its broad array of services and to build new relationships—and in the process increase revenue. "Collaboration is crucial for Baker McKenzie," says Colin Murray, the firm's North America CEO. Because the partners know they will be asked to provide examples of collaboration in their year-end memos, they have an incentive to work with other lawyers across the firm throughout the year. Since switching to a collaborative approach six years ago, Baker McKenzie North America has increased its revenue more than 40 percent.[14]

Measuring Activator behaviors

As an industry, professional services firms are notoriously guilty of focusing on lagging indicators like billable hours, utilization, contract value, firm rankings, and Net Promoter Score to manage their businesses. If a firm is pursuing an Activator journey, many of those outcome metrics will improve, but most of the measures themselves won't change. Instead, firms will see bookings and contract value, rankings, and other traditional measures improve. The biggest difference firms will see is in the *way* business is won—that it will be more team-based rather than individual, less likely to be in response to an inbound inquiry and less prone to go through RFP.

But what about leading indicators? Here, we recommend that firms leverage tools and technology they likely already have in place rather than inventing a new set of Activator indicators that will require additional investment or process.

For instance, most firms use time-tracking software to keep tabs on billable hours, engagement resourcing, and utilization. As we already know, Activators spend more time on business development than non-Activators, and firms should expect to see an uptick in reported business development time from professionals trained on Activator behaviors. CRM can also provide some insight into leading indicators: Are professionals entering more client opportunities and logging more interactions with their clients? And, of course, for those firms that have invested in tools like LinkedIn's Sales Navigator, this is a great way for firms to gain a deeper understanding of whether their professionals are connecting broadly and creating value for clients. Finally, tools like Intapp's

DealCloud can evaluate interactions between professionals, prospects, clients, and other third parties to build a detailed picture of the strength of each relationship. This can be invaluable to leaders who are eager to understand not just how professionals are engaging the outside market but also how much they're collaborating with their colleagues inside the firm to deliver value to clients.

Beyond data from existing platforms, a great way for firms to assess whether their professionals are starting to head down the Activator path is adjusting client feedback surveys to surface this data. Most surveys we see tend to be fairly generic, gauging satisfaction with the firm and its professionals and likelihood to engage again in the future. Firms that are on an Activator journey, however, should cast a broader net with their surveys to understand not just whether work was completed to the client's satisfaction but the way in which professionals engaged with the client. For instance:

- Did our professional bring you new ideas proactively or only respond with ideas when asked?

- Did our professional deliver the business impact and outcomes you expected?

- Did our professional deliver the work in the manner you expected?

- Did our professional do anything to help support your personal goals and objectives?

- Did our professional engage with you individually or did they collaborate with others from our firm to deliver value?

- Did our professional engage with you exclusively or with your broader team?

Most client surveys are designed in large part to gauge clients' satisfaction with the firm and the work its professionals have completed. To generate leading indicators, however, we recommend a version of these instruments be deployed to prospective clients as well, with obvious modifications to the suggested questions.

One final recommendation on leading indicators is that firms take advantage of our Activator Diagnostic, which is a truncated version of the original survey used in our research.[15] This diagnostic takes roughly ten to fifteen minutes for a professional to complete and produces a number of powerful insights for professionals and leaders—for instance, an overall Activator Score as well as benchmarks for a number of commit, connect, and create behaviors and habits. Having deployed the diagnostic to thousands of partners and associates from a wide range of professional services firms, we've found that it produces a reliable normal distribution—in other words, about 20 percent of professionals score near the bottom, 20 percent near the top, and the remainder clustering around the firm's mean Activator Score. With a scale of 0–100, our guidance is as follows: 75 or above is excellent; 60–74 is above average; 45–59 is average; 30–44 is below average; and below 30 is poor.

Across the several thousand who have taken the diagnostic to date, the average score is 46. Newly promoted partners, lateral hires from government, and associates, of course, tend to score significantly lower given their relative lack of business development experience. Firms on an Activator journey have found this diagnostic to be a useful tool for targeting training investments as well as a weathervane to provide firm leaders with a set of leading indicators for whether Activator behaviors are starting to take root.

Leading Activator Change

Driving change and making it stick in a professional services firm is hard. In her book *Leading Professionals*, Laura Empson—a professor at Bayes Business School at City, University of London—explains that "Individual professionals—highly educated, highly intelligent, and highly opinionated—are generally reluctant to see themselves as followers. . . .

They value their autonomy and confer authority on their leaders on a highly contingent basis."[16]

As years of research have shown, selling is a skill like any other. To improve, it requires focus, repetition, and practice. But how do firms drive improvement when their professionals can opt in or out of the journey and business development tends to get crowded out by other responsibilities? By making business development effectiveness a singular focus—or Wildly Important Goal—for the firm.

The concept of Wildly Important Goals, or WIGs, was coined by Chris McChesney, Sean Covey, and Jim Huling in their book *The Four Disciplines of Execution.*[17] The authors discuss how the "whirlwind" of day-to-day business operations tends to get in the way of making progress against long-term goals. The pull of the urgent task forces focus away from the new goal and back toward old behaviors. In professional services firms, this often means that client work and pressing project requirements end up distracting partners from other objectives leaders have asked them to focus on—such as becoming an Activator firm.

Aside from the whirlwind of everyday business, leaders themselves often compound the problem by asking their teams to focus on too many priorities. These tend to be internal priorities, and firms often fall into the trap of creating strategies that are built from the inside out rather than client in. Most leaders want their teams to do more, and consequently, the pile of goals grows to be unmanageable or unintelligible over time. "One prime suspect in execution breakdown," McChesney, Covey, and Huling write, "was clarity of the objective: People simply didn't understand the goal they were supposed to execute. In fact, in our initial surveys, we learned that only one employee in seven could name even one of their organization's most important goals. . . . The other 85 percent named what they *thought* was the goal, but it often didn't remotely resemble what their leaders had said."[18]

To overcome this challenge, these authors argue, successful organizations declare a *very* small set of objectives—typically no more than two or three—to be their WIGs. These WIGs should be large, compelling, and difficult to achieve—in other words, they should be objectives that cannot be met without significant and focused attention. They should also be specific, measurable, and time-bound. For example, "Double the revenues of our health-care practice by the end of the year." Or "Increase our average Activator Score by 20 percent across the firm by the second quarter of next year."

A great example of the power of making business development improvement the WIG of the organization—and the impact it can have—comes from the law firm Hogan Lovells.

When he was elected CEO of Hogan Lovells in July 2020, Miguel Zaldivar quickly concluded that the firm was not yet achieving its full potential and needed to transform the way it went to market. The firm had grown between 5 percent to 7 percent annually, but that was largely due to realizing rate increases, with overall demand remaining consistently flat. To grow organically, it had to start taking more work from competitors, and for that to happen, it would be imperative for all its partners to become more proactive, entrepreneurial, and collaborative in their business development efforts.

"Some of our partners grew up being told that they only needed to do good work and client business would follow," Zaldivar explains, "But in today's market, that's not enough. We had to continue to be excellent lawyers but also get out there and not rely just on our reputation and brand. We had to start being more proactive. We had to start selling and doing it as a team. It was the only path to sustainable growth." Client feedback echoed the need to engage differently in the market. As Ina Brock, the Managing Partner for Clients & Industries at that time and now the sales transformation lead and a senior life sciences and litigation partner in Munich, told us, "We're known as a 'nice' firm with 'nice' people who deliver excellent client service. But we also don't like to bother clients and really engage with them between matters. Clients were telling us if we were more proactive and 'hungry,' we'd win more work."

Zaldivar's most important goal was to accelerate profitable revenue growth and make Hogan Lovells a top five firm in their five core sectors by focusing on cross-selling, institutionalizing client relationships, and improving pitch win rates from 24 percent to over 40 percent. To accomplish this, the firm needed partners to become more ambitious and more supportive of one another. "Becoming more ambitious," Zaldivar explains, "means being hungrier, more proactive, and more confident in telling clients what we can do for them. But we wanted partners to also be more supportive in their business development approach. We didn't want a bunch of ambitious individuals. We wanted our people hunting in teams. We wanted them sharing origination credit and feeding one another work."

One of the keys to getting a firmwide transformation like Activator to stick is to task specific working groups with the responsibility of driving action internally. This is exactly what Hogan Lovells did when they convened their Strategic Sales Group. Initially comprising thirty of the firm's top rainmakers, it served as a working group that collectively owns the firm's stated growth goal, taking an active role in identifying needs and opportunities across the firm, and developing training programs on sales best practices that can help the firm attain its objectives.

Over the past few years, the Strategic Sales Group has identified and executed on several new programs in support of their growth goal, including:

- A firmwide Sales Academy, which is also embedded into the firm's existing training and development programs, including for new partners, counsel, and senior associates, among others.

- A Win of the Week Series that celebrates pitch wins or teams that have demonstrated recent sales success. This is supplemented with a New Business Award Program, which offers discretionary bonuses for those below partner level who introduce a new client or unearth a net-new cross-sell opportunity within an existing client account. The combination "makes very clear to every person who works here that you're not expected to sit behind a desk and write memos," says Brock. "It's a mindset we want to cultivate— getting everyone out talking to people and feeling like part of the process of generating work."

- A Pitch to Win approach that includes a "pitch mentor" deployed from the Strategic Sales Group for the most strategically important pitches. The mentor's role is to act as an independent advisor and sounding board to the team throughout the pitch process. As Brock explains, "We used to put all our energy into preparing pitch materials. Now we're much more focused on engaging key client stakeholders from day one to understand their needs and making sure we're differentiated by putting the best team and solution in front of the client and preparing for the client-facing elements of the pitch process."

- Pitch to Win also leveraged a new opportunity engagement and qualification process called Ready-Set-Go, which ensures a fast start on new pitches. Within the first forty-eight hours of learning about a new opportunity, key partners from across the firm are mobilized and empowered to think strategically about whether to pursue the opportunity and, if so, how to win the business. Some of the criteria the group considers are the existence of conflicts, whether the company is an existing client of the firm or has the potential to be a growth opportunity for the firm, whether it's work that leverages Hogan Lovells' core strengths and areas of expertise, and whether it's work that Hogan Lovells has a good shot of winning.

Hogan Lovells takes a long-term view on the impact of the sales transformation program—expecting that it won't completely pay off for five to ten years. But within the first four years, it's already paying huge dividends. Win rates have increased from 24 percent in 2019 to above 48 percent from 2021 to 2023. And, what's more, there's been a complete mindset shift internally as lawyers have seen the payoff from the investments the firm made in their commercial success. "By any metric, we have already succeeded: revenue per lawyer, demand growth, profitability, and win rates," says Zaldivar. "But, more importantly, we've become a completely different firm. We're hungrier, more proactive, more confident, and more collaborative than ever."

Summary

In the doer-seller world of professional services, where professionals navigate the chaotic day-to-day demands on their time, asking for behavior change requires leaders to put forth a compelling vision, communicated with clarity and aligned on a single goal everyone can rally around. It also calls for the need to align all firm-level resources and activities—such as hiring and partner selection to training, enablement, and rewards—to this vision.

Absent a clear vision and communications, many firms on an Activator journey will struggle to drive sustainable behavior change. As McDermott's Elizabeth Gooch says, "Consistency and discipline is a key part of sales and professionals may struggle to balance selling with their primary focus of delivering excellence in client work. Meaningful improvements can only happen when leaders are willing to articulate the need for all partners to focus on growth, saying 'This is our direction, and we're going to invest in it and put real resources behind it." Or, as Dr. Larry Richard succinctly put it, "If you're ever going to achieve something when you're introducing something new, you have to understand the principles of defusing resistance."

Conclusion

A Powerful Reset

Before a recent Activator training workshop we were delivering to a group of new partners, we were invited to sit in to listen to a panel of the firm's senior leaders as they took questions from the group. All seemed to be going smoothly until one of the newly minted partners saw an opportunity to put the senior leaders on the spot about what he perceived to be a noncollaborative culture across the firm.

"How are we supposed to build our own books of business when the senior partners won't let us in?" he complained. "We talk about collaboration all the time, but the firm seems to look the other way when it comes to the behavior of our top rainmakers." What ensued was a lively debate about culture, incentives, and rewards. Only by making—or by paying—the firm's top partners to share their clients with their colleagues would collaboration actually happen, this new partner cohort seemed to conclude. But then the firm's managing partner—who had been quiet until this point—spoke up and asked a question that seemed to startle the group and immediately redirect the conversation: "Have any of you brought one of these senior partners to a client of yours?"

She shared a personal story to illustrate what she meant. Many years earlier, when she was a new partner herself, she was preparing for a client pitch with a group of colleagues and noticed that there was an opportunity to showcase the firm's capabilities in an area adjacent to the work being proposed and for which the firm had market-leading capabilities.

The issue, however, was that the firm's best-known partner in this space was also notoriously difficult to collaborate with. For many years, he'd built his book of business around a small set of key client relationships, which he managed to turn into some of the firm's biggest-paying clients. Attempts by other partners to earn an introduction to one of his clients were routinely shot down and no amount of encouragement from the firm's senior leaders that he should try to bring the breadth of the firm's capabilities to his clients seemed to make a difference. It had become an accepted fact among the firm's partners that these were *his* clients, not the *firm's* clients. "The team was pretty dead set against inviting him to join us for the pitch meeting. And it was hard to blame them," she said, "But I managed to convince them that there was more to be gained by including him than by excluding him and that it represented a great opportunity to differentiate against one of our biggest competitors—one that we were going up against for the work."

"So," she said, "I decided to swing by his office to explain the client situation and ask him if he would be open to joining our team for the pitch. I think he just about fell out of his chair," she said to the amusement of the new partners in the room. "You see," she explained, "as a young partner myself, I also thought the deck was stacked against me, and I remembered feeling the same level of anxiety as you are right now about breaking into big client accounts that were owned by much more experienced and accomplished partners. But I learned pretty quickly that being helpful and generous with colleagues—and not expecting anything in return—was the best way to build trust and goodwill and to lay a foundation for collaboration." She went on to share that her team not only beat out their competitor for the client's business but also managed to carve out a big chunk of work for their sharp-elbowed colleague. "And wouldn't you know it," she said, "not two weeks later, he rang me up and asked if I wanted to travel to New York with him to meet some of his clients so that I could share some of the work I'd been doing with other clients in my field. Today, those are some of my deepest client relationships, and that partner and I have collaborated on dozens of big opportunities together. So, be proactive, be generous, and be helpful and good things will follow."

In many respects, this managing partner's story is a perfect explanation for why Activators do the things that they do. It's not simply because they know it's a more effective way to develop business in a world of decreasing client loyalty. To a person, what they'll tell you is that the real reason they do what they do is because it enables them to forge deeper, more valuable relationships with colleagues and clients alike. Above all, Activators pride themselves on being *helpful* to others. And while this sounds simple, it's a powerful reset for many professionals who are focused on things like compensation plans, industry rankings, or other accolades. And it isn't just Activators telling us this. The data bears it out as well. Statistically, the single most impactful variable in our entire study was how professionals responded to the following statement: "My clients seek out my advice even when we're not engaged in paid work." Nearly 60 percent of Activators report that their clients do this compared to only 37 percent of non-Activators.

Skeptics might shrug and say this is just free work and, of course, what client doesn't like free work? In fact, many firm leaders expressly forbid or at least discourage their professionals from doing any work for clients that isn't billable. But herein lies the crux of what makes an Activator approach different from that of a typical professional. Whereas most non-Activators start with paid work that offers them an opportunity to deliver value and, potentially, earns them the right to develop a deep relationship with their client, these steps flow in almost reverse order for Activators. Activators *start* by delivering value, which forges a stronger, trust-based relationship with the client. These relationships aren't built on invoices, but on the professional's fundamental desire to be helpful to the client and deliver value, *irrespective* of whether the client pays them for it.

Because Activators lead with value, they build a broader, more stable, and resilient foundation in their client relationships. Put simply, the more a professional *activates,* the more value they create for clients and the more business they generate for themselves and their firms.

The perfect illustration of the difference between Activators and other professionals is in how they land new business. All professionals pitch for new business. When the average professional does this, they spend a significant amount of time credentialing themselves and their firms. Why? Because, in most cases, the client has only a vague idea of who the professional is and what they and their firm is capable of. For most professionals, a pitch has a binary outcome: the business is won or lost. But Activators don't pitch for business so much as they evolve their relationship with the client. Engaging in paid work is the natural culmination of the value they've already delivered and the investment they've already made in the client relationship. Paid work is just the next step. Not surprisingly, 80 percent of Activators report that when they discuss paid work with clients, they focus on what they can do for the client in the future as opposed to what they've delivered to other clients in the past. Only 63 percent of non-Activators reported that this was their approach. Activators don't need to lead with their credentials because the client already knows who they are, the client already trusts them, and there is already a relationship in place. The same can't be said for other professionals who see the pitch as the *beginning* of the client relationship.

For many firms and professionals, the new client buying environment will be a difficult landscape to navigate. But for top professionals who are able to adapt their business development approaches for this reality, it presents an opportunity to dislodge long-entrenched incumbent providers and grow their books of business. "The door has started to open," said one Activator from a global consultancy, "This is true of my clients as well, but I would prefer the door is open because there is more to be gained by me walking through than to be lost if others walk through my clients' doors. We may have lost our unique privilege, but we've gained a wide playing field of opportunity."

Appendix

Study Methodology

A project like this is no small undertaking and goes through numerous phases before conclusions are reached.

The first step is to build a study model that "chalks the field" for the research. What are we studying (*dependent* variable) and what do we think affects the thing we're studying (*independent* variables)? In our case, we were studying business development effectiveness of professionals. The things that could affect it are variables such as time spend, attitudes, skills, behaviors, and use of technology tools, among others. In all, our team settled on a set of 108 different variables we hypothesized might have an impact on a professional's individual business development effectiveness (see figure A-1).

The next step is to generate a set of hypotheses as to how the different independent variables might affect the dependent variable. To do this, our team scoured several decades' worth of books and articles on professionals and what makes for an effective business developer. What emerged was a set of themes that helped us document the conventional wisdom around professional services business development. We also reflected on our own previous work in B2B sales. We'd spent the better part of twenty years studying B2B salespeople and had a deep understanding

Quantitative model

108 total attributes

Client communications
- Reasons for initiating contact
- Frequency of contact

Qualification criteria
- Strategic fit with our offerings
- Client budget

Events
- Event attendance
- Preparation and follow-up

Time allocation
- Business development vs. client work
- Time across client journey

Social networking tech
- Use of LinkedIn
- Approach to social networking

Client loyalty
- Strength of relationship
- Client expectations

Pitch meetings
- Use of pitch materials
- Pitch meeting strategy

Business development strategy
- Emphasis on expertise
- Pushing client thinking

Firm support of BD
- Customer relationship management and marketing tools
- Knowledge management

Client interactions
- Focus on past vs. future
- Deepening relationships

Demographics
- Professional specialty
- Country/region
- Years of experience
- Size of book
- Gender
- Age

Control variables

+

Performance measures
- Percent of available incentive maximum compensation
- Generating revenue for the firm
- Generating revenue from new clients
- Generating additional revenue from existing clients
- Generating revenue for areas of the firm other than his/her own practice area
- Effectiveness at business development vs. client-related work

Factor analysis
- Extraction method: Principal component analysis
- Rotation method: Varimax with Kaiser normalization

Regression analysis
- Compared factors to performance ratings
- Regressed all variables against outcomes

= Profile of top rainmakers

of what made the very best different from the rest. So we tested a number of these behaviors as well—in part to settle, once and for all, the question of how different doer-sellers really are from actual salespeople.

Then we needed to figure out how to test these hypotheses in a survey that was challenging enough so as not to be gameable while at the same time not being so burdensome and difficult that a busy professional would refuse to complete it. Our survey ended up taking the average professional about forty-five minutes to complete. Importantly, the survey instrument itself used a variety of question types, including Max-Diff, an approach that forces respondents to trade off between different bundles of options. The common refrain from professionals who completed it was that the survey wasn't straightforward—that it forced them to be quite introspective and to think critically about how they go about business development. Put simply, there were no easy or obviously right answers. Finally, to make sure the dataset was clean, we checked for and eliminated any instances of straightlining (i.e., when a respondent demonstrates a pattern of question response that indicates they are simply trying to get through the survey as quickly as possible).

Our survey collected detailed information on the business development strategies, techniques, attitudes, time spend characteristics, and tool and resource use of nearly 3,000 partners from across all the major subsegments of professional services—namely, consulting, law, and accounting—as well as several other niche segments like investment banking, PR/communications, executive search/talent advisory, and commercial real estate. Participating firms ran the gamut from some of the biggest global players in their segments to smaller boutique outfits and represented a broad range of geographic markets, from North America to Europe, Latin America, Asia-Pacific, and Australia-New Zealand.

The survey gave us our independent variable set. To provide a dependent or outcome variable, we then asked the leaders of the forty-one firms that participated to assess each professional's business development effectiveness relative to their peers on a range of standard business development dimensions. We asked firm leaders to score each rep on a scale on questions such as:

- How effective is this individual, compared with his/her peers in the firm, on overall business development?

- How effective is this individual, compared with his/her peers in the firm, on landing new clients?

- How effective is this individual, compared with his/her peers in the firm, on expanding existing clients?

- How effective is this individual, compared with his/her peers in the firm, on collaborating with colleagues to expand the firm's business footprint with clients?

Our model also included a set of control variables—for instance, age, gender, tenure, geographic market, and professional specialty—to ensure the findings would be broadly generalizable.

Using this dataset, we performed a few types of statistical modeling, the results of which we shared in chapter 1. This included a factor analysis (which looks for how variables group together to describe different business development approaches) and a regression analysis (which looks at how each of the variables we tested impacts business development effectiveness). In addition to our quantitative analysis, we also conducted hour-long behavioral interviews with more than eighty top performers from across our sample population. These interviews proved to be pivotal to our study. Where the statistical analysis showed us *what* top performers do differently, the interviews revealed the *how* and the *why* behind their approach to business development.

Comparing Descriptive and Predictive Results

How do we reconcile the results of the regression that show that there is only one approach positively correlated with performance and this analysis that shows there are other ways to be a top rainmaker?

First, in the regression, we are looking at a pure comparison of the attributes associated with each profile. But remember, in real life, no professional is 100 percent of any one profile. While each professional majors in one of the five approaches to business development, they also have elements—sometimes significant, sometimes trace—of the other four. So the descriptive analysis compares professionals by the profile they major in and confirms what the regression shows us: those who pursue an Activator approach are disproportionately more likely to be high performers—and disproportionately less likely to be low performers than any other profile.

But how can a professional who spikes in one of the other, non-Activator profiles still be a top rainmaker? After all, the regression didn't show that these approaches were unproductive; it showed that they were *counterproductive*—negatively correlated with business development performance. The simple explanation is that those top-performing Realists, Confidants, Debaters, and Experts almost certainly also possess a healthy dose of Activator, which balances out the negative impact of their primary approach. A more nuanced explanation is that when we look at the statistically significant variables that factored together to describe the different profiles, some of the variables in each were significantly positive while others were significantly negative. For those non-Activator rainmakers, it stands to reason that they've managed to avoid the attributes of their primary approach that are negatively correlated with performance. In other words, a high-performing Confidant likely has a healthy dose of Activator skills but also is applying the Confidant approach in a careful way to avoid stepping on the landmines that overall tend to drive the negative performance associated with that approach. They are executing a losing approach at an extremely high level and have managed to make it work for them.

A golf swing is a good analogy: most instructors agree that there is a right way and a wrong way to swing a golf club. But there are plenty of players who manage to score well and perform at a high level while not demonstrating a "classic" swing. And most golfers can rattle off the names of professionals they've seen on TV whose swings look like anything but what the textbooks prescribe. And yet, they are competing with—and often winning against—the best players in the world.

A Note on Statistical Validity

The results of the regression analysis, in particular, surprises many professionals because of how stark the results are. It's therefore worth taking a moment to assure readers of the validity of these results.

Recall that the survey instrument measured a comprehensive list of more than one hundred attitudes, activities, and time spend, as well as demographic factors. By casting such a broad net, we were able to deal with the possible concern that there is something impacting performance that we didn't measure. Next, we loaded the survey data onto profiles using factor analysis, which happened very cleanly, and was aided by our use of MaxDiff, which forced respondents to make tradeoffs. The profile scores are not correlated with one another, allowing us to more easily isolate the impact of each (that is, the regressions were clean with low multicollinearity across profile scores). And we tested and controlled for demographic factors such as years of experience, age, region, professional specialty, and so forth.

We collected the performance data that we used as our dependent variable, which was provided by the participating firms, not the partners who completed the survey. Participating firms did not have access to individual responses. We then normalized this performance data by firm to account for firms that may systematically over- or underrate the performance of their partners relative to other firms.

The analysis showed an extremely strong, statistically significant relationship between the profile scores and revenue generation performance. All of the regressions were at least 95 percent significant except for the Realist, which is not unusual since that profile has a modest impact on performance. In particular, the regression of the Activator score on revenue generation performance was 99.9999999 percent significant—that is to say, 1 in 300 million odds of the results coming from random chance, which provides strong evidence for the effectiveness of the Activator approach.

Notes

Introduction

1. See Kate Wolstenholme et al., *Annual Law Firms' Survey 2023: Bold Steps to Sustainable Transformation*, PwC, 2023, 12, https://www.pwc.co.uk/industries/legal-professional-business-support-services/law-firms-survey/2023.html.

Chapter 1

1. Thomson Reuters Institute and Georgetown Law Center on Ethics and the Legal Profession, *2024 Report on the State of the US Legal Market: The Challenge of Targeting the Right Markets with the Right Offerings*, 2024, 28, https://www.thomsonreuters.com/en-us/posts/legal/state-of-the-us-legal-market-2024/.

2. Matthew Dixon and Brent Adamson, *The Challenger Sale: Taking Control of the Customer Conversation* (New York: Penguin/Portfolio, 2011); Brent Adamson, Matthew Dixon, Pat Spenner, and Nick Toman, *The Challenger Customer: Selling to the Hidden Influencer Who Can Multiply Your Results* (New York: Penguin/Portfolio, 2015); Matthew Dixon and Ted McKenna, *The JOLT Effect: How High Performers Overcome Customer Indecision* (New York: Penguin/Portfolio, 2022).

3. Clayton M. Christensen, Dina Wang, and Derek van Bever, "Consulting on the Cusp of Disruption," *Harvard Business Review*, October 2013.

Chapter 2

1. This passage is excerpted from Matthew Dixon et al., "What Today's Rainmakers Do Differently," *Harvard Business Review*, November–December 2023.

2. Excerpted from Dixon et al., "What Today's Rainmakers Do Differently."

3. Paul J. Zak, *The Moral Molecule: How Trust Works* (New York: Plume, 2013).

4. Sam B. G. Roberts and Robin I. M. Dunbar, "Managing Relationship Decay: Network, Gender and Contextual Effects," *Human Nature* 26, no. 4 (2015): 426–450.

5. Dee Gill, "New Study Disavows Marshmallow Test's Predictive Powers," *UCLA Anderson Review*, February 24, 2021.

6. James Clear, *Atomic Habits: Tiny Changes, Remarkable Results: An Easy and Proven Way to Build Good Habits and Break Bad Ones* (New York, Avery, 2018); Charles Duhigg, *The Power of Habit: Why We Do What We Do in Life and Business* (New York: Random House, 2012).

7. James Clear, "The Five Triggers That Make New Habits Stick," https://jamesclear.com/habit-triggers.

8. Roy F. Baumeister et al., "Ego Depletion: Is the Active Self a Limited Resource?," *Journal of Personality and Social Psychology* 74, no. 5 (1998): 1252–1265.

9. James Clear, "How to Build New Habits by Taking Advantage of Old Ones," https://jamesclear.com/habit-stacking.

10. Clear, "How to Build New Habits by Taking Advantage of Old Ones."

11. Clear, "The Five Triggers That Make New Habits Stick."

12. Clear, "The Five Triggers That Make New Habits Stick."

13. Nicholas A. Christakis and James H. Fowler, "The Spread of Obesity in a Large Social Network over 32 Years," *New England Journal of Medicine* 357, no. 4 (2007): 370–379.

14. Clear, "The Five Triggers That Make New Habits Stick."

15. Philippa Lally et al., "How Habits Are Formed: Modeling Habit Formation in the Real World," *European Journal of Social Psychology* 40, no. 6 (2010): 998–1009.

16. James Clear, "How to Stop Procrastinating on Your Goals by Using the 'Seinfeld Strategy,'" https://jamesclear.com/stop-procrastinating -seinfeld-strategy.

17. Clear, "How to Stop Procrastinating on Your Goals."

18. The concept of the habit loop has been popularized in books like Clear's *Atomic Habits*, Duhigg's *The Power of Habit*, and Nir Eyal's *Hooked: How to Build Habit-Forming Products* (New York: Penguin/Portfolio, 2014).

Chapter 3

1. Matthew Dixon et al., "What Today's Rainmakers Do Differently," *Harvard Business Review*, November–December 2023.

2. Dixon et al., "What Today's Rainmakers Do Differently."

3. Brent Adamson et al., *The Challenger Customer: Selling to the Hidden Influencer Who Can Multiply Your Results* (New York: Penguin/Portfolio, 2015), 38.

4. Heidi K. Gardner's research is considered by most to be the definitive work on collaboration in professional services. Readers interested in learning more should start with two of her most widely referenced pieces: "When Senior Managers Won't Collaborate: Lessons from Professional

Services Firms," *Harvard Business Review*, March 2015; and *Smart Collaboration: How Professionals and Their Firms Succeed by Breaking Down Silos* (Boston: Harvard Business Review Press, 2017).

5. Gardner, *Smart Collaboration*, 31.

6. Gardner, "When Senior Managers Won't Collaborate," 4.

7. Gardner, "When Senior Managers Won't Collaborate," 4.

8. Gardner, "When Senior Managers Won't Collaborate," 5.

9. Robin Dunbar, "Neocortex Size as a Constraint on Group Size in Primates," *Journal of Human Evolution* 22, no. 6 (June 1992): 469–493.

10. Dale Purves et al., *Principles of Cognitive Neuroscience*, 1st ed. (New York: Sinauer Associates, 2007).

11. Robin Dunbar, *How Many Friends Does One Person Need? Dunbar's Number and Other Evolutionary Quirks* (New York: Faber & Faber, 2010).

12. Robin Dunbar, *Grooming, Gossip, and the Evolution of Language* (Cambridge, MA: Harvard University Press, 1998).

13. Pádraig MacCarron, Kimmo Kaski, and Robin Dunbar, "Calling Dunbar's Numbers," *Social Networks* 47 (2016): 151–155.

14. Fiona Coward and R. I. M. Dunbar, "Communities on the Edge of Civilization," in *Lucy to Language: The Benchmark Papers*, ed. Robin I. M. Dunbar, Clive Gamble, and J. A. J. Gowlett (Oxford, UK: Oxford University Press, 2014), 380–406.

15. R. A. Hill and Robin I. M. Dunbar, "Social Network Size in Humans," *Human Nature* 14 (2002): 53–72, courses.washington.edu/ccab /Hill%20and%20Dunbar%202003%20-%20Group%20size.pdf.

16. Robin Dunbar and Richard Sosis, "Optimising Human Community Sizes," *Evolution and Human Behavior* 39, no. 1 (2018): 106–111.

17. Dunbar, *How Many Friends Does One Person Need?*

18. Jim Rutt, "Robin Dunbar on Friendship," *The Jim Rutt Show*, transcript of episode 140, podcast audio, September 14, 2021, jimruttshow .blubrry.net/the-jim-rutt-show-transcripts/transcript-of-episode-140 -robin-dunbar-on-friendship.

19. Mark S. Granovetter, "The Strength of Weak Ties," *American Journal of Sociology* 78, no. 6 (1973): 1360–1380.

20. MIT Sloan School of Management, "A Team of MIT, Harvard and Stanford Scientists Finds 'Weaker Ties' Are More Beneficial for Job Seekers on LinkedIn," press release, September 15, 2022, mitsloan.mit.edu /press/a-team-mit-harvard-and-stanford-scientists-finds-weaker-ties-are -more-beneficial-job-seekers-linkedin.

21. Markus Baer, "The Strength-of-Weak-Ties Perspective on Creativity: A Comprehensive Examination and Extension," *Journal of Applied Psychology* 95 (2010): 592–601.

22. LinkedIn Insights data, April 2024.

23. Equilar, Inc., internal data.

24. Sheon Han, "You Can Only Maintain So Many Close Friendships," *The Atlantic*, May 20, 2021, https://www.theatlantic.com/family/archive/2021/05 /robin-dunbar-explains-circles-friendship-dunbars-number/618931/.

25. Brent Adamson, Matthew Dixon, and Nick Toman, "The End of Solution Sales," *Harvard Business Review*, July–August 2012; Gartner research cited in Garin Hess, "Bust the Bottleneck: Win B2B Sales More Often by Applying the Theory of Constraints," *Forbes*, November 17, 2021.

26. For a full discussion of this research, see Adamson, Dixon, and Toman, "The End of Solution Sales"; Adamson et al., *The Challenger Customer*.

27. Adamson et al., *The Challenger Customer*.

28. Adamson, Dixon, and Toman, "The End of Solution Sales"; Adamson et al., *The Challenger Customer*.

29. Adamson, Dixon, and Toman, "The End of Solution Sales"; Adamson et al., *The Challenger Customer*.

30. Adamson et al., *The Challenger Customer*.

31. Adamson, Dixon, and Toman, "The End of Solution Sales." This finding has been validated in multiple follow-on studies. Researchers at Forrester, for instance, found that nearly 74 percent of B2B buyers completed most of their research online before completing an offline purchase (see Lori Widzo, "Myth Busting 101: Insights into the B2B Buyer Journey," Forrester, May 25, 2015, https://www.forrester.com/blogs/15-05-25-myth _busting_101_insights_intothe_b2b_buyer_journey/).

Chapter 4

1. This passage is excerpted from Matthew Dixon et al., "What Today's Rainmakers Do Differently," *Harvard Business Review*, November–December 2023.

2. David H. Maister, Charles H. Green, and Robert M. Galford, *The Trusted Advisor* (New York: Free Press, 2000).

3. "Understanding the Trust Equation," Trusted Advisor, n.d., https://trustedadvisor.com/why-trust-matters/understanding-trust/understanding -the-trust-equation, accessed November 12, 2024.

4. Ashley Reichheld and Amelia Dunlop, *The Four Factors of Trust: How Organizations Can Earn Lifelong Loyalty* (Hoboken, NJ: Wiley, 2022).

5. For more on how top performers overcome the agency dilemma in client relationships, see Matthew Dixon and Ted McKenna, *The JOLT Effect: How High Performers Overcome Customer Indecision* (New York: Penguin/Portfolio, 2022).

6. Jody Padar, LinkedIn, https://www.linkedin.com/feed/update/urn:l i:activity:7182727841283756032/.

7. Philip Lay, Todd Hewlin, and Geoffrey Moore, "In a Downturn, Provoke Your Customers," *Harvard Business Review*, March 2009.

8. Lay, Hewlin, and Moore, "In a Downturn, Provoke Your Customers."

9. Matthew Dixon and Brent Adamson, *The Challenger Sale: Taking Control of the Customer Conversation* (New York: Penguin/Portfolio, 2011).

10. Dixon and Adamson, *The Challenger Sale*, 47.

11. For more on how to build and leverage insight, see Matthew Dixon and Brent Adamson, *The Challenger Sale*; and Brent Adamson et al., *The*

Challenger Customer: Selling to the Hidden Influencer Who Can Multiply Your Results (New York: Penguin/Portfolio, 2015).

12. Adamson et al., *The Challenger Customer*, 67.

13. Dixon and Adamson, *The Challenger Sale*, 56–59.

14. Dixon and Adamson, *The Challenger Sale*, 56.

15. Mike Schultz and John E. Doerr, *Insight Selling: Surprising Research on What Sales Winners Do Differently* (Hoboken, NJ: Wiley 2014).

16. The discussion of Grainger is adapted from Matthew Dixon and Brent Adamson, "The Worst Question a Salesperson Can Ask," hbr.org, October 7, 2011, https://hbr.org/2011/10/the-single-worst-question-a-sa. For a full discussion of the Grainger case, see Dixon and Adamson, *The Challenger Sale.*

17. Dixon and Adamson, *The Challenger Sale*, 58.

18. For more litmus tests like these, see Adamson et al., *The Challenger Customer*, 69–70.

Chapter 5

1. Gary R. VandenBos, ed., *APA Dictionary of Psychology*, 2nd ed. (Washington, DC: American Psychological Association, 2015).

2. VandenBos, *APA Dictionary of Psychology.*

3. For more on self-determination theory, see Richard M. Ryan and Edward L. Deci, *Self-Determination Theory: Basic Psychological Needs in Motivation, Development, and Wellness* (New York: The Guilford Press, 2017).

4. Lizzy McLellan, "Lawyers Reveal True Depths of Mental Struggles," ALM/Law.com, February 19, 2020, https://www.law.com/2020/02 /19/lawyers-reveal-true-depth-of-the-mental-health-struggles/.

5. Helen Riess, *The Empathy Effect: Seven Neuroscience-Based Keys to Transforming the Way We Live, Love, Learn, and Connect across Differences* (Louisville, CO: Sounds True, 2018).

6. Zak Kelm et al., "Interventions to Cultivate Physician Empathy: A Systematic Review," *BMC Medical Education* 14, article 219 (2014), https:// bmcmededuc.biomedcentral.com/articles/10.1186/1472-6920-14-219.

7. Helen Riess, "Empathy Training for Resident Physicians: A Randomized Controlled Trial of a Neuroscience-Informed Curriculum," *Journal of General Internal Medicine* 27, no. 10 (October 2012): 1280–1286.

8. Riess, "Empathy Training for Resident Physicians."

9. Daniel H. Pink, *To Sell Is Human: The Surprising Truth about Moving Others* (New York: Riverhead Books, 2012).

10. Pink, *To Sell Is Human.*

11. Ibrahim Senay, Dolores Albaraccín, and Kenji Noguchi, "Motivating Goal-Directed Behavior through Introspective Self-Talk," *Psychological Science* 21, no. 4 (2010): 499–504.

12. Martin Seligman, *Learned Optimism: How to Change Your Mind and Your Life* (New York: Vintage, 2006). For a broader summary of this research, see Pink, *To Sell Is Human.*

13. Martin Seligman and Peter Schulman, "Explanatory Style as a Predictor of Productivity and Quitting among Life Insurance Agents," *Journal of Personality and Social Psychology* 50, no. 4 (1986): 832–838.

14. Seligman, *Learned Optimism*.

15. Dr. Larry Richard, interview by Mary O'Carroll, *Pearls On, Gloves Off: The Legal Ops Podcast*, July, 26, 2022, https://podcasts.apple.com /us/podcast/4-dr-larry-richard-explains-lawyer-personalities-and /id1620908192?i=1000567266115.

16. Richard, interview.

Chapter 6

1. For more on how to use a ROPE calculation in an insight-based message, see Matthew Dixon and Brent Adamson, *The Challenger Sale: Taking Control of the Customer Conversation* (New York: Penguin/Portfolio, 2011).

2. "The Gentle Science of Persuasion, Part Four: Consistency," *W. P. Carey News*, January 17, 2007, news.wpcarey.asu.edu/20070117-gentle -science-persuasion-part-four-consistency.

3. Chip Heath and Dan Heath, *The Power of Moments: Why Certain Experiences Have Extraordinary Impact* (New York: Simon and Schuster, 2017).

4. Clay Halton, "Zone of Possible Agreement (ZOPA): Definition in Negotiating," Investopedia, September 25, 2021, www.investopedia.com /terms/z/zoneofpossibleagreement.asp#; James Chen, "Best Alternative to a Negotiated Agreement (BATNA)," Investopedia, July 6, 2023, www .investopedia.com/terms/b/best-alternative-to-a-negotiated-agreement -batna.asp#.

5. PON staff, "Power in Negotiation: The Impact on Negotiators and the Negotiation Process," *Daily Blog*, Program on Negotiation at Harvard Law School, January 26, 2024, www.pon.harvard.edu/daily/negotiation -skills-daily/how-power-affects-negotiators.

6. Katie Johnson, "The Art of Haggling," HBS Working Knowledge, May 7, 2012, hbswk.hbs.edu/item/the-art-of-haggling.

7. Adam D. Galinsky, William W. Maddux, Debra Gilin, and Judith White, "Why It Pays to Get Inside the Head of Your Opponent: The Differential Effects of Perspective Taking and Empathy in Negotiations," *Psychological Science* 19, no. 4 (2008).

8. Matthew Dixon and Brent Adamson, "Why Your Salespeople Are Pushovers," hbr.org, October 11, 2019, hbr.org/2011/10/why-your-sales people-are-pusho.

9. PON staff, "Power in Negotiation."

10. Rebecca J. Wolfe and Kathleen L. McGinn, "Perceived Relative Power and Its Influence on Negotiations," *Group Decision and Negotiation* 14, (2005): 3–20.

11. Helen Lee Bouygues, "Don't Let Anchoring Bias Weigh Down Your Judgment," hbr.org, August 30, 2022, hbr.org/2022/08/dont-let-anchoring -bias-weigh-down-your-judgment.

12. PON staff, "In a Price Negotiation, Should You Make the First Offer?," Program on Negotiation at Harvard Law School, *Daily Blog*, February 27, 2024, www.pon.harvard.edu/daily/business-negotiations/in-a-price-negotiation-should-you-make-the-first-offer.

13. Chris Voss, *Never Split the Difference: Negotiating as If Your Life Depended on It* (New York: HarperBusiness, 2016).

14. Noah J. Goldstein, Steve J. Martin, and Robert B. Cialdini, *Yes! 50 Scientifically Proven Ways to Be Persuasive* (New York: Free Press, 2009).

15. Goldstein, Martin, and Cialdini, *Yes!*

16. Daniel Kahneman and Amos Tversky, "Prospect Theory: An Analysis of Decision under Risk," *Econometrica* 47, no. 4 (1979): 263–291.

17. Robert B. Cialdini, "Commitment and Consistency: Hobgoblins of the Mind," in *Influence: The Psychology of Persuasion* (New York: Harper-Business, 2007), 57–113.

18. Joseph Schwarzwald, Ahron Bizman, and Moshe Raz, "The Foot-in-the-Door Paradigm: Effects of Second Request Size on Donation Probability and Donor Generosity," *Personality and Social Psychology Bulletin* 9, vol. 3 (1983), 443–450.

19. Voss has written extensively on the power of fairness in negotiations. See, for example, Chris Voss, "An FBI Hostage Negotiator Teaches You the 'F' Word in Negotiations," September 9, 2014, Black Swan Group blog, https://www.blackswanltd.com/newsletter/2014/09/an-fbi-hostage-negotiator-teaches-you-the-f-word-in-negotiations/.

20. Lindsay Willott, "The Service Recovery Paradox," Customer Thermometer, January 30, 2020, https://www.customerthermometer.com/customer-retention-ideas/the-service-recovery-paradox/.

21. Roy Lewicki and C. Wiethoff, "Trust, Trust Development, and Trust Repair," in *The Handbook of Conflict Resolution: Theory and Practice*, ed. Morton Deutsch and Peter T. Coleman (San Francisco: Jossey-Bass, 2000), 86–107.

22. Admittedly, there is some skepticism about how honest clients will be in feedback calls. Asking for feedback is necessarily injecting a level of conflict into the interaction. According to Chris Argyris, the late Harvard professor and founder of the body of work called *productive interactions*, there are three strategies people can use in situations of conflict: (1) bypass—avoid discussing the issue and move on; (2) name—note the problem, but don't discuss it; and (3) engage—actually discuss the problem. The risk to the relationship is higher as you move up that scale, so people tend to employ bypass in most situations (see Geoff Tuff, Steve Goldbach, and Elizabeth Lascaze, "How to Get Honest and Substantive Feedback from Your Customers," hbr.org, September 15, 2023, https://hbr.org/2023/09/how-to-get-honest-and-substantive-feedback-from-your-customers). Research shows that it is important to ask for the feedback in a way that is vulnerable. Indeed, research shows that it may be better to ask for advice for next time, rather than feedback about what could have gone better (see Jaewon Yoon et al., "Why Asking for Advice Is More Effective Than Asking for Feedback,"

hbr.org, September 20, 2019, https://hbr.org/2019/09/why-asking-for-advice
-is-more-effective-than-asking-for-feedback).

23. Cialdini, "Reciprocation: The Power of Give and Take . . . and Take," in *Influence: The Power of Persuasion*, rev. ed. (New York: HarperCollins, 2007), 17–56.

24. David B. Strohmetz et al., "Sweetening the Till: The Use of Candy to Increase Restaurant Tipping," *Journal of Applied Social Psychology* 32, no. 2 (2002): 300–309.

Chapter 7

1. Our "Anatomy of the Activator Firm" is a simple framework that firm leaders can use to understand the key attributes of an Activator firm, assess their firm's capabilities against those attributes, and prioritize areas for improvement. For more information, see https://www.dcminsights.com/activatoranatomy.

2. Matthew Dixon et al., "What Today's Rainmakers Do Differently," *Harvard Business Review*, November–December 2023.

3. This passage is excerpted from Dixon et al., "What Today's Rainmakers Do Differently."

4. This passage is adapted from Dixon et al., "What Today's Rainmakers Do Differently."

5. Edward L. Deci and Richard M. Ryan, *Intrinsic Motivation and Self-Determination in Human Behavior* (New York: Plenum Press, 1985); Daniel H. Pink, *Drive: The Surprising Truth about What Motivates Us* (New York: Riverhead Books, 2009).

6. Ethan Bernstein and Cara Mazzucco, *Winning Business at Russell Reynolds (A)*, Case 422-045 (Boston: Harvard Business School Publishing, March 2022, rev. May 2022).

7. Bernstein and Mazzucco, *Winning Business at Russell Reynolds (A)*.

8. Bruno Bolzan, interview by the authors, February 29, 2024.

9. Clarke Murphy, interview by the authors, January 31, 2024.

10. Bernstein and Mazzucco, *Winning Business at Russell Reynolds (A)*.

11. Bernstein and Mazzucco, *Winning Business at Russell Reynolds (A)*.

12. Bernstein and Mazzucco, *Winning Business at Russell Reynolds (A)*.

13. This passage is adapted from Dixon et al., "What Today's Rainmakers Do Differently."

14. This passage is adapted from Dixon et al., "What Today's Rainmakers Do Differently."

15. For more information about the Activator Diagnostic, see https://www.dcminsights.com/activator-diagnostic.

16. Laura Empson, *Leading Professionals: Power, Politics, and Prima Donnas* (Oxford, UK: Oxford University Press, 2017).

17. Chris McChesney, Sean Covey, and Jim Huling, *The Four Disciplines of Execution: Achieving Your Wildly Important Goals* (New York: Free Press, 2012).

18. McChesney, Covey, and Huling, *The Four Disciplines of Execution*, 5.

Index

Acknowledgments

This project had its roots in a series of conversations our research team had with the leadership team at Intapp, the leading provider of cloud software to professional and financial services firms. What started as a casual discussion of opportunities to do some cobranded marketing suddenly turned into something much bigger. With the enthusiastic support of Intapp's cofounder and Chief Product Officer, Thad Jampol, and Chief Marketing Officer, Scott Fitzgerald, we sketched out a plan for what would become the "Rainmaker Genome Project" and would ultimately result in an article in *Harvard Business Review* and then a book published by Harvard Business Review Press.

From the very beginning, we found a set of kindred spirits at Intapp—people who were as passionate and curious as we were about insight generation and the opportunity to explore—and maybe debunk—some of the age-old conventional wisdom in the professional and financial services industries. While we owe Intapp a huge debt of gratitude for the critical financial support they provided, we are actually more thankful for their intellectual partnership over the past three years. At every step of the way, the Intapp team leaned in, recruiting their clients to participate in the study, giving us feedback on our hypotheses and research deliverables, and providing us with a platform to road test our findings with industry leaders. In every respect, Intapp was the perfect research partner. It's no exaggeration to say that this study would never have gotten off the ground were it not for our partnership. We see Intapp continuing with the same passion to pursue ways they can build on what we have learned. With that in mind, we also wish to thank CEO and Chairman John Hall, as well as a host of other Intapp leaders, including Ben Harrison, Beth Cuzzone, Laura Saklad, Matthew Hardcastle, Gemma Prescott, Laura Herlihy, Ali Robinson, and Miki Hanlen, just to name a few. We would also like to sincerely thank former Intappers, Lavinia Calvert, Cindy Koluch, Guy Adams, and Mark Holman, as well as Intapp strategic advisor and board member, Ralph Baxter, for their tremendous efforts in supporting this project from start to finish.

Our research team at DCMi is small but mighty. In addition to the coauthors of this book, we would like to thank our head of quantitative research, Kevin Acker, and strategic research advisor, Lara Ponomareff, for their invaluable contributions to this project. An additional group of staff members played direct roles in the production of this book, notably Ethan Dixon, who produced all of the graphics, Oscar Channer, who supported us during editing rounds, and Carter Lynn and Georgia Beatty, who oversaw our data-collection efforts. And finally, while we were working on the research and the book, we were supported by a tremendous team of professionals who kept the DCMi business not only humming along but firing on all cylinders: Alex Low, Matt Kelly, Amanda Andrade, Phil Sofia, Jill Forbes, Ging Dimalanta, Pat Spenner, Sylwia Jenner, Zoe Kosoff, and Lorelei Domke.

While we don't share the names of our clients, we would be remiss in not extending a huge thank you to all of the firms around the world who have trusted us with their business. We've had the great privilege of working with some of the most progressive executives and professionals across dozens of leading law, consulting, accounting, executive search, public relations, investment banking, and commercial real estate firms. We can say with all sincerity that every time we've delivered our program to them, it has been an experience in which we've learned just as much as we've taught.

Pulling a book together is no small feat and only happens with the support of many industry professionals. This book was expertly stewarded by such world-class talents as our agent, Jill Marsal, of Marsal-Lyon; our editors at Harvard Business Review Press, Kevin Evers and Juan

Martinez; HBR design director, Stephani Finks; production editor, Anne Starr; and our publicists, Mark Fortier and Norbert Beatty of Fortier Public Relations. Together, they helped turn our research into a compelling, thoughtful, and well-constructed story that we hope professionals and company leaders will find value in for many years to come.

Projects like this one exact the greatest toll on those closest to you. They are asked to put up with long nights and weekends of work, missed holidays, and work-filled vacations. And so, last but not least, we wish to thank our spouses—Amy Dixon, Jill Channer, Alison McKenna, and Mark Freeman—as well as our children—Aidan Dixon, Ethan Dixon, Norah Dixon, Clara Dixon, Oscar Channer, Hugh Channer, Will McKenna, Ella McKenna, Anna Freeman, and Sarah Freeman—for their unwavering love, patience, and support.

About the Authors

MATTHEW DIXON is a founding partner of DCM Insights (DCMi), a training and consulting firm that uses data and research-backed frameworks to help professional services firms implement an Activator approach to business development. Prior to cofounding DCMi, he held leadership roles in research, product, and advisory at a variety of companies, including CEB (now Gartner), Korn Ferry, and Tethr (now Creovai).

Known for his groundbreaking research, Dixon is recognized as one of the world's foremost experts in sales, business development, marketing, and client experience. He has coauthored some of the most important business books of the past decade, including *The Challenger Customer*; *The Challenger Sale*, which has sold over a million copies worldwide and been translated into more than a dozen languages; *The Effortless Experience*; and *The JOLT Effect*. He is a frequent contributor to *Harvard Business Review*, with more than twenty print and online articles to his credit, including several articles that appear in the HBR 10 Must Reads series book *HBR's 10 Must Reads on Sales*.

Dixon holds a PhD from the Graduate School of Public and International Affairs at the University of Pittsburgh, as well as a BA in international studies from Mount St. Mary's University in Maryland. He and his family currently reside in the Washington, DC, area.

RORY CHANNER is a founding partner of DCMi. Prior to cofounding DCMi, he held executive leadership positions in marketing, business development, and sales at McDermott Will & Emery, Ruffalo Noel Levitz, RealizedCare, CEB (now Gartner), Portrait Software (now part of Pitney Bowes), and Business Genetics.

Channer has a consistent track record of improving organizational growth curves. Originally trained as an industrial psychologist, he brings science and his twenty-five-plus years of commercial experience to the professional services sector. Not only has he helped numerous law firms boost growth, he has personally trained several hundred firm partners on improving their client engagement skills.

Channer holds both a BSc (Hons) and a postgraduate diploma in industrial psychology from the University of Hull in England and postgraduate qualifications in leadership coaching and counseling from George Washington University in Washington, DC, and Regent's University London. He and his family currently reside in Northern Virginia.

KAREN FREEMAN is a partner at DCMi, where she's responsible for product and delivery. She has spent her career in data analytics, research, and teaching. Before joining DCMi she was the global head of digital and analytics learning at McKinsey & Company. In that role she led a team in upskilling roughly seventeen thousand consultants globally in topics including advanced analytics modeling, leading digital transformations, agile methodology, and design thinking.

Prior to her work at McKinsey, Freeman spent thirteen years at CEB (now Gartner) in research and in learning and development roles. There she led three best-practice membership organizations, developing insights, advice, and benchmarks for Global 1000 functional heads in marketing, sales, and customer service. Much of the company's highest-impact research was spearheaded by the teams she led. Several articles about this research were published in *Harvard Business Review* and later became the subject of two bestselling business books, *The Challenger Sale* and *The Effortless Experience*.

Later, as head of CEB University, a department within CEB, Freeman oversaw development and delivery of over a thousand training sessions for more than ten thousand participants worldwide in sales, insight and advisory, and corporate roles. She also spent several years as executive director of research at the Advisory Board for the Arts, a research and best practices organization for nonprofit arts organizations. In addition, she is currently on the board of Signature Theatre in Arlington, Virginia.

Freeman has an AB from Harvard University and an MBA from MIT. She currently lives in Northern Virginia with her family.

TED McKENNA was a founding partner of DCMi and is the cofounder and CEO of SellingInnovations, a research-based training, enablement, and advisory company supporting business-to-business commercial organizations. A coauthor of the bestselling book *The JOLT Effect*, Ted is an accomplished researcher whose work has appeared in the pages of *Harvard Business Review*. He is also a sought-after speaker and advisor to sales, business development, and customer experience teams around the world.

Ted is an expert in analyzing behaviors—of customers, doer-sellers, frontline sales and service teams, leaders, and board members—and applying analytics in various forms of content, products, and services. The study featured in *The JOLT Effect*, one of the world's largest studies of sales ever conducted, mined 2.5 million sales calls using advanced data science and leading AI/ML tools to build models, predictive scores, and behavioral frameworks. Previous studies called for deploying syndicated research methods to mine more-structured sources, such as survey, interview, demographic, and jobs data, including research contained within the bestselling book *The Challenger Sale*.

Prior to cofounding DCMi, Ted held numerous executive leadership positions in product, strategy, research, advisory, and enablement for Tethr (now Creovai), Russell Reynolds Associates, and CEB (now Gartner).

Ted holds a BA in economics from the University of Iowa and resides with his family in the Chicago area.